UNIVERSITY LIBRARY
UW-STEVENS POINT

W9-CNY-057

doing business with
Slovenia

GLOBAL MARKET BRIEFINGS

doing business with
Slovenia

CONSULTANT EDITOR:
JONATHAN REUVID

**KOGAN
PAGE**

London and Sterling, VA

Publisher's note

Every possible effort has been made to ensure that the information contained in this handbook is accurate at the time of going to press, and the publishers and authors cannot accept responsibility for any errors or omissions, however caused. No responsibility for loss or damage occasioned to any person acting, or refraining from action, as a result of the material in this publication can be accepted by the editor, the publisher or any of the authors.

First published in Great Britain and the United States in 2004 by Kogan Page Limited

Apart from any fair dealing for the purposes of research or private study, or criticism or review, as permitted under the Copyright, Designs and Patents Act, 1988, this publication may only be reproduced, stored or transmitted, in any form, or by any means, with the prior permission in writing of the publisher, or in the case of reprographic reproduction in accordance with the terms of licences issued by the Copyright Licensing Agency. Enquiries concerning reproduction outside those terms should be sent to the publishers at the undermentioned addresses:

120 Pentonville Road   22883 Quicksilver Drive
London N1 9JN   Sterling VA 20166-2012
UK   USA
www.kogan-page.co.uk

© Kogan Page and individual contributors, 2004

ISBN 0 7494 4074 0

British Library Cataloguing in Publication Data

A CIP record for this book is available from the British Library

Library of Congress Cataloging-in-Publication Data

Doing business with Slovenia / consultant editor Jonathan Reuvid.
    p. cm.
Includes index.
    ISBN 0-7494-4074-0
    1. Slovenia--Commerce. 2. Slovenia--Commercial policy. 3. Slovenia--Economic conditions. 4. Investments, Foreign--Slovenia. 5. Industrial laws and legislation--Slovenia. I. Reuvid, Jonathan. HF1578.7.D65 2004
330.94973--dc22
                                    2003026274

Typeset by JS Typesetting Ltd, Wellingborough, Northants
Printed and bound in Great Britain by Thanet Press Ltd, Margate

K
3826.4
.D64
Slovenia

Contents

CELJE BROKERAGE HOUSE

✦ Limited company with shortage of the name CBH Ltd. was established by two previous members of Ljubljana Stock Exchange (The "Ljubljanska banka splosna banka Celje", now "Banka Celje d.d." and the "RC IRRI d.o.o. Celje). CBH started operating in September 1993. The founding capital of 14 million SIT was purchased by 11 founders in 1993.

✦ Today the registered capital of CBH Ltd. is 190 million SIT. The company is owned by 2 companies and 12 individuals. The largest owners are: ETOL d.d., FILBA d.o.o. President of the Supervisory Board is Mr. Boris Mihelčič, B. Sc. Ec., general manager of FILBA d.o.o. The headquarters of the company are on Vrunceva street 1 in Celje.

✦ CBH is a member of the Ljubljana Stock Exchange (LJSE) and Central Securities Clearing Corporation (KDD).

✦ Our basic activities are trading with securities by order of and on behalf of the client (Stock Brokerage), management of assets by order of and behalf of the client (Asset management), and analysis. Quick and most of all quality response of the stockbrokers is the key to clients satisfaction and trust. CBH employs seven active brokers.

✦ On-line trading via internet is the best solution for everyday trading. This safe service is provided by our information system which includes a range of useful analytic tools with historical data for all listed securities accessible on our web page.

- As a member of KDD we can provide our clients additional services, related to securities: ownership transfer, pledge of securities, transfer based on inheritance.

- In May 2002, after another LJSE member Ebrokers Ltd. ended with brokerage services, CBH included all its clients and employees. At the same time CBH started with a branch office in Ljubljana. The Ljubljana branch office is located in the new Eurocenter building, together with other important financial institutions such as KDD, Central Securities Clearing Corporation.

- As an authorised participant on the securities market CBH provides investing in NAV of several Slovenian mutual funds.

- Until 6/2003 we have gained more than 60.000 clients. We started with 5 employees, until August 2003 the number increased to 14.

- The sum of clients assets increased to 145 mio €.

Fact sheet:
- Date of establishment: 1993
- The company is registered in the court register at the District Court in Celje, No. 1/5677/00
- Capital: 0,8 mio €
- Main activity: J 67.120 Brokerage with securities
- Legal form: Private Limited company
- Tax ID number: 75358450
- Management Board: Mr. Zdenko Podlesnik and Mrs. Darja Orozim
- President of the Supervisory Board: Mr. Boris Mihelčic

C B H

d. o. o., Celje

CELJSKA BORZNO - POSREDNIŠKA HIŠA

Vrunčeva 1, 3000 Celje

Tel.: 03/ 425 20 00
Fax: 03/ 425 20 20

Poslovna enota LJUBLJANA

Tivolska 48
1000 Ljubljana
Tel.: 01/ 300 70 00
Fax: 01/ 300 70 07

http://www.cbh.si

Foreword

Slovenia is aiming at becoming an active and successful competitor in the global economy, whose competitive strengths will be based on high-value-added manufacturing and services, quality, innovation and entrepreneurship. Greater international competitiveness, however, is not a goal in itself. It ensures high economic growth, which in turn ensures a strong and prosperous country with high quality of life and social welfare. Therefore, the Slovenian government is determined to create conditions for strong and sustainable growth, based on an internationally competitive economy. We firmly believe that the enlarged entrepreneurial platform Slovenia will gain by becoming a full EU member is an important vehicle for achieving this goal.

The internationalization of the Slovenian economy is an important determinant of sustainable growth and, therefore, direct foreign investment – inward or outward – is gaining in importance. While Slovenia's outward investment is mainly concentrated in the countries of the former Yugoslavia and to a certain extent in transition countries, the inward investment originates mainly from EU countries. Over the past years inward investment to Slovenia has surged and ties to other countries are being steadily built and reinforced.

Thanks to a well-educated workforce with a good command of foreign languages, Slovenia has all the attributes of a top destination for smaller knowledge economy projects, high-tech centres, distribution and logistic hubs, and call centres. I am also convinced that the cutting edge of Slovenia's small and open economy is its short response time to demand, the flexibility of its business community and its excellent industrial tradition, as well as numerous contacts around the globe. I do not doubt this is a mix of qualities that make Slovenia an interesting business partner.

Tea Petrin, PhD
Minister of the Economy

List of Contributors

The Bank Austria Creditanstalt Group is responsible for the markets in Central and Eastern Europe (CEE) within the HVB Group, Europe's third largest banking group. Bank Austria Creditanstalt is Austria's largest commercial bank and one of the leading banking groups in the East. This is reflected in a comprehensive network of banking subsidiaries, representative offices and other financial services companies.

Within the HVB Group the economics department of Bank Austria Creditanstalt is competent for the entire macro- and microeconomic research for Austria and the CEE region. In fulfilling these tasks, the department coordinates the data provided by and made available to the economic research units of the group's CEE subsidiaries. It is also the EU competence centre for lobbying and for questions on eastward enlargement.

Coface is the world number one in export credit insurance and insurance business rating. It is also a leader in the provision of credit information, drawn from its network of offices and partnerships and from a unique database, updated in real time, of 35 million companies. Active in both traditional and business-to-business (B2B) enterprises, Coface has been involved in the development of international trade for over 50 years.

Deloitte & Touche Central Europe spans 17 countries and has 27 offices, but they operate as one cohesive entity. In 1997 Deloitte & Touche integrated their national practices to form Deloitte & Touche Central Europe because they realized that to best serve their clients they needed to be able to share their knowledge and human resources throughout the whole of their geographical area. Their integration has allowed them to manage centrally and deliver locally, adding value to their services and allowing them to be performed in the most efficient manner. In becoming one firm, they positioned themselves as the professional services firm to beat.

Deloitte & Touche Central Europe has the expertise and cultural diversity that is necessary to provide world-class services in the 21st century. In addition to all the resources they have to draw on within Central Europe, they also have the expertise of their global organization,

Celje Fair

The largest fair and event house in Slovenia

CELJSKI SEJEM

www.ce-sejem.si

Celje Fair is a company responsible for organising fairs and events with some 35 years tradition and big reputation in Slovenia and abroad. It is one of the largest Slovenian enterprises of its kind. Its core business activity is organising fair events and its side activity organisation of other related events such as congresses, seminars, cultural events, entertaining events, humanitarian, commercial, sports and many other. Together with its daughter company Step d.o.o. Maribor (100% ownership) the Celje Fair is the organiser of 22 annual and biennial events and over 300 other events take place every year. Its premises offer hospitality to half a million of visitors, participants and guests.

Around 60,000 square metres of exhibition halls

The Celje Fair boasts a number of features such as modern and up-to-date infrastructure. Its exhibition halls measure 60,000 square metres, of which there are 39,000 square metres of indoor and 21,000 square metres of outdoor exhibit locations of high standard. It also has the most modern hall (hall L) in Slovenia which offers 10,000 square metres of exhibit locations with all the necessary infrastructure. This attractive hall built in 1999 is of great interest to exhibitors and organizers.

There is an adjoining carpark which offers more than 2000 parking spaces which can be expanded to 5000 in the vicinity during the biggest fair event, International Trade Fair (ITF). Exhibition halls are located close to the access to Ljubljana Maribor motorway, only a kilometre away. Its central position is a big advantage when it comes to organising events and welcoming visitors from all over Slovenia and abroad.

Seating capacity from 16 to 1,200 seats

In addition to 22 fair events the Celje Fair organises numerous other events. In the past few years it has increased its capacity with the newly-built and updates premises suitable for supporting activities such as consultations, meetings, lectures, presentations, days of congress, banquets, parties, concerts, dances, to name but a few. This kind of events and congress activities have 7 session rooms with the seating capacity between 16 to 1,200 seats at its disposal in the Celje Fair Centre, with all the necessary infrastructure, technical equipment and other capacities catering for food and drink offer.

CELJSKI SEJEM d.d.
Dečkova 1, 3102 CELJE, SLOVENIA
Telephone: ++386 3/5433-000
Telefax: ++386 3/5419-164
E-mail: info@ce-sejem.si
net: www.ce-sejem.si

MOS

…e central fair event organised by the Celje Fair is

…TERNATIONAL TRADE FAIR (ITF),

…e largest and most visited event.

…re than 1,700 exhibitors and 175,000 visitors

…t only is ITF the largest fair event organised by the Celje …r, but also the largest event in Slovenian space and among … largest of its kind in Europe. Every year this is a venue for …00 exhibitors (32 countries took part in the last one) and …und 175,000 visitors came to view its 60,000 square metres …exhibition halls.

… programme is very comprehensive and it comprises …tallurgical, electrotechnical activities, woodworking, the …d industry and furniture making, construction and …ecommunications activities. We must not forget banking, …urance agencies, electrical goods and consumer goods on …play.

…er 100 accompanying events with renown …-organisers

…t only is ITF important because of its display programme, …t also because of all the accompanying events which are …epared by the Celje Fair together with the following co-…ganisers: Chamber of Craft of Slovenia, Slovenian Chamber …Trade and Commerce, the Ministry of Economy, the Centre …r Small Business Promotion, local Entrepreneurship Centre …d many more. Accompanying events such as consultations, …und tables, lectures, entertaining and informative events …count for more than 100 events every year.

…e largest Slovenian commercial and media event …f September

…portant co-organisers with their up-to-date themes …ditionally contribute to ITF credibility and its reputation of …siness fair and one of the most important commercial and …edia events which takes place in Slovenia every September. …t only is the Fair an outstanding business opportunity but …so an opportunity for socialising and informal get-together …ere most noticeable Slovenian public and political figures …eet.

International Fairs in 2003 in Celje:

03

20th - 23rd March

8th fair FLORA
gardening, floristry and landscape architecture

6th fair DOMOFIN
finishing building, construction and renovation

7th fair EKO (biennial fair)
ecology and environmental protection

8th - 11th April

7th FORMA-TOOL* (biennial fair)
tools, toolmachines

5th PLAKGEM* (biennial fair)
plastics, rubber and chemistry

1st GRAFIKA (biennial fair)
graphics, paper, tools, raw material and maschinery for graphics

10th - 17th September

36th ITFC (MOS) International Trade Fair
(largest fair and business event in Slovenia)

27th - 28th September

3rd fair HAIR AND BODY BEAUTY**
haidressing an cosmetics fair

8th - 11th October

1st PROTECTION (biennial fair), specialised fair
focused on rescue, protection and security

International Fairs in 2004 in Celje:

04

11th - 14th March

14th Fair CAR AND MAINTENANCE
(biennial fair), auto service, repair industry, cars

6th MOTO BOOM Fair (biennial fair)
motocycles and equipment for motorcyclists

4th Exhibition of UTILITY VEHICLES
(biennial fair), commercial vehicles

5th Fair LOGOTRANS* (biennial fair)
logistics and transportation

25th - 28th March

9th fair FLORA
gardening, floristry and landscape architecture

18th - 21st May

12th ENERGETIKA Fair* (biennial fair), energetiscs,
energetical sources, economical use of energy

11th TEROTECH Fair* (biennial fair)
maintenance, cleaning, building renovation

29th - 30th May

4th fair HAIR AND BODY BEAUTY**
haidressing and cosmetics

8th - 15th September

37th ITFC (MOS) International Trade Fair
(largest fair and business event in Slovenia)

* Organizer is STEP d.o.o., member of the Celje Fair group
** Co-organizer is Hair fashion magazine

Deloitte Touche Tohmatsu. As part of Deloitte Touche Tohmatsu, their clients are given the same high level of services that they provide, anywhere in the world.

Dr Roman Glaser, Perutnina Ptuj Chairman of the Board of Directors, PhD, VMD, was born on 11 July 1947 at Ptuj. In 1972 he graduated from the Veterinary Faculty of the University in Ljubljana, in 1982 he was awarded a master's degree, and in 1987 he was awarded a PhD in veterinary sciences. In 1988 he came from the Ptuj Drava Region Institute for Veterinary Science and Animal Husbandry to Perutnina Ptuj, and was appointed a member of the Managing Board, responsible for the reconciliation and development of production-technological affairs. In 1989 he became the Vice-Chairman of production and in 1992 the Chairman of the public enterprise, and in September 1997 the Supervisory Board of Perutnina Ptuj d.d. appointed him the Chairman of the Board of Directors. He was granted the Chamber of Commerce of Slovenia award for exceptional economic and entrepreneurial achievements for 1996.

He actively participates in managing boards of the Chamber of Commerce of Slovenia, and is the Supervisory Board Chairman of Probanka Maribor, the Supervisory Board Chairman of Perutnina Ptuj, Pipo Cakovec Company, Bistra Research Institute Chairman of the Council, Chairman of Perutnina Ptuj Cycle Club. He was appointed the Perutnina Ptuj Chairman of the Board of Directors until 25 August 2007.

Viktor Lence is President of the Board of Postna Banka Slovenije d.d.

The Merchant International Group Limited (MIG) is an international security and intelligence-gathering group, working across 140 countries. MIG undertakes bespoke product work globally and serves many international corporate clients. The primary mission of MIG is to identify, quantify and manage the risks associated with overseas investments. MIG looks at the world differently and thereby provides its clients with intelligence and insight, expanding the options available to them.

Janus Orban is Technical Director of Varstroj d.d.

Robert Otorepec is Assistant Manager of Fairs at Celjski Sejem d.d., the leading Slovenian trade fair organizer. He graduated from the Faculty of Economics and Business of Maribor University in 1995 and in marketing the following year. Robert was appointed to his present position in 2000.

Celjski Sejem organizes eight or nine international trade fairs and several local fairs each year. It is also concerned with the organization of cultural, entertainment and sports events and the renting out of convention halls. The most important event at its 60,000 m² fairgrounds in Celje is the annual International Trade Fair involving over 1,600 exhibitors from 30 countries which attracts 175,000 visitors.

Pavle Pensa is a senior partner of Jadek & Pensa, a leading Ljubljana-based Slovenian corporate and commercial law firm, featured in *European Legal 500* journal. The firm advised on the privatization of a 39 per cent share in Nova Ljubljanska Banka and also acted for Lek, the Slovenian pharmaceutical company, on its acquisition by Novartis.

Biljana Radonjic is a senior analyst at Civilitas Research, the Cyprus-based international political and economic consultancy.

Jonathan Reuvid graduated in economics from Oxford and was employed as an economist by the French national oil company, Total, at the time of its UK market entry. From there he moved into investment banking, financial consultancy and marketing strategy. After seven years working for a US multinational engineering group with European general management responsibility, he engaged in the development of joint ventures and technology transfers in northern China. In 1989, Jonathan embarked on a new career in business publishing, editing and writing a series of international business books with Kogan Page. He has a keen interest in the delivery of adult learning on the Internet.

TIPO is the Slovenian Trade and Investment Promotion Agency under the Ministry of the Economy of the Republic of Slovenia.

Upon graduation in the field of marketing at the University of Maribor (Slovenia), **Jani Toros** pursued his career in different fields of marketing. Years of advertising agency experience led to marketing director positions in two major Slovenian publishing companies. Working for the second publishing company expanded his role and he was asked to establish and build a new sales promotion department. The success of the newly built department pushed him into establishing his own marketing and advertising agency, where, as the owner, he also took a general manager position. It was his work through his own company that brought him into marketing in the food processing industry. As an account director for projects that involved food processing companies he was later offered a marketing director position for one of his clients – one of largest food-producing companies in Slovenia. For the past 10 years he has been focusing on food-processing industry marketing and is currently a marketing and sales adviser to the board of directors of Mlinotest, another important food-producing company in the Slovenian market.

Portrait of HINCO Lendava d.o.o.

HINCO Lendava d.o.o.
Kolodvorska 43
9220 Lendava
Tel: +386 2 5789 030
Fax: +386 2 5789 040
Email: hinco@hinco.si
http://www.hinco.si

Business Data:

Type of organization:	Limited Liability Company
Size:	Medium
Property:	Private
Registration Number:	5641276
Tax Number:	55066747
Founding Capital:	30.875.000,oo Sit (ab. 150.000 US$)
Founders:	Hajdinjak Jo?ef, Hajdinjak Djurdja, Hajdinjak Mitja
Market share:	0,51 %

Strategic Goal

It is of great importance for us that our clients and business associates form a favourable opinion about our company. We strive for developing successful business relations with our partners and offer to them:

"High quality goods at a competitive price, with personal attention and perfect service."

History and Activities

HINCO traces its history back to 1992 when HINCO Lendava d.o.o., Slovenia was founded as a trading, manufacturing and consulting company. The founder, Mr. Jöef Hajdinjak, has taken up the challenge of leading his own company, after many years of work experience in Refinery Lendava and INTERINA Budapest.

The main business activities of the company:

1. HINCO Wholesale trade
2. HINCO Candle production
3. HINCO Consulting services

Today HINCO Lendava d.o.o., as a part of the HINCO GROUP system, is fully capable for complying with its customers' wishes, as for supplying with crude oil products, slack wax (extra), paraffin, base oils, kerosene, intermediaries and other petrochemicals. We are present mainly on East and Central European markets.

We have excellent business relations with our partners from Germany, Denmark, Poland, Russia, Ukraine, Belarus, Romania, Hungary, Sweden, Slovakia, Czech Republic, Austria, The Netherlands, Croatia, Serbia and Monte Negro and others.

Those who have already established business contacts with us and are acquainted with our services and products know that we offer quality at a competitive price and correct, in time delivery.

Business System - HINCO GROUP
- The success of the company is shown in its activities, which have extended day by day and have resulted in a line of affiliated and associated companies:
- HINCO Lendava d.o.o. – Slovenia, International Headquarters of HINCO GROUP for trading in crude oil, crude oil products, petrochemical products in Central and East Europe, consulting and engineering in refineries and petrochemical plants, candle production and WEB solutions.
- HINCO Kft Budapest – Hungary, Trading in crude oil, crude oil products and petrochemical products in Central and East Europe. Import/Export to/from Hungary.
- HHINCO d.o.o. Belgrade – Trading company covering markets of Serbia and Monte Negro and Bosnia and Herzegovina
- HHINCO Representative Office Moscow – Russia, Presenting HINCO GROUP in Russia and former CIS countries. Consulting and engineering on this market.
- HHINCO International llc - Washington, Trading, financial transactions, and consulting activities.

www.hinco-group.com

1. HINCO Wholesale Trade
The main business activity of HINCO is trading in secondary refinery products and petrochemicals on the Central and East European markets.

HINCO Lendava does business with the companies within HINCO GROUP and partnership companies in Russia, Hungary, Poland, Croatia, The Netherlands, Slovakia, Serbia and Monte Negro, Romania and Ukraine.

The primary product assortment includes import, export of several products, which are handled by following operating groups:

Paraffin wax
Selection of fully refined to semi refined paraffin in slabs, flakes, powder or liquid as per Buyers production process requirement.

Slack wax
Different types and origins of Slack Wax for Paraffin Wax production.

Base Oil
Industrial oils, Base oils and additives for Base oil production

Petrochemicals
Products for lacquer and dye industry, intermediaries, polymers, PVC, carbon black,…

Crude oil products
Vacuum Gas oil, Virgin Naphtha, Lighting Kerosene,

We can say with pleasure that through the years of acting in the trading business, we created together with our partners long-term cooperation relationships, which entitle our motto in trading:

" CREATING BUSINESS TOGETHER"

2. HINCO Production
With the intention of splitting the business risks, we have additionally started with our own candle production. According to the fact that we have successfully traded in slack wax and paraffin wax it was the only logical step to invest in to the production using paraffin wax as the basic material for candle production.

HINCO Lendava d.o.o. today manufactures various kinds of paraffin candles in a manufacturing plant in Lendava.

Our range of candles includes the following candles of various dimensions and colours:

- garden party lights
- long-burning candles for outdoor and indoor illumination
- scented candles for air fragrance and mosquito repellent candles
- cemetery candles
- decorative candles of various shapes and sizes
- candles for floral arrangements
- table candles for home and restaurants
- festive and ceremonial candles
- candle gift set

Stylish designed candles, packed in high-quality packing can serve the most pretentious customer. The most important thing is to satisfy the requirements of our customers with our products, which will be competitive on the market.

Our aim is to conclude cooperation with wholesalers and to develop with them a long-term cooperation in the field of candles. We are also prepared and have the possibility to develop and produce candles, which are not in our production range at the moment; with other words, we align our production with buyer's request, like we are selling already to many Western and Eastern European Countries.

We are always available to offer further information about our products and can promise personal attention whenever is required. This service is given to all our customers and this fact alone bear our reputation in candle production, which has been established for 6 years and made our motto:

"Illuminate your moments!"

3. HINCO Consulting Services

As a team our mission is to help companies to strengthen relations with their clients and business contacts, to increase their business efficiency and to find new opportunities for marketing and trading their products and services.

Our consulting and study scope include:

1. Trade Consulting:
   - Market research,
   - Feasibility Study,
   - Commercial partner research
   - Sales and distribution networks creation
   - Promotion and advertising
   - On-spot negotiation assistance
   - Assistance to fairs and exhibitions

2. International Representation

Representing your Company in Slovenia and former Yugoslavia can avoid many of the shortfalls, costs and issues associated with short-term representation. It helps international businesses overcome troublesome time zone differences and, of course, avoids the issue of the time taken to get on-site in the event of serious problems. Also you can use advantage of our Market knowledge

3. Internet Consulting

For the already existed WEB pages we offer:

- Consulting in advertising, introduction of innovations, how to attract more visitors, satisfied customers ...

For New WEB pages:

- Concept and planning
- Development and writing of the content
- Graphic and program solutions

- Maintenance and refreshing of WEB pages
- Expanding and redesigning of WEB pages
  (from static to dynamic+e-shops).

HINCO.net

Business goals have not changed, but the way of doing business has changed greatly. Clients simply expect more information, a wider range of products and services and stronger support. The companies have to react to these changes innovatively and HINCO.NET can help them to find a solution. We work closely with our clients in order to meet their requirements, achieve their goals and implement their ideas.

With the whish to obtain our experiences in internet we designed new B2B marketplace to help companies find business partners all over the world, and to gather more experience in the new era of e-commerce.

http://b2b.hinco.biz

Hinco.biz focuses on business-to-business of different products. All producers, end-users, importers, exporters and other professionals can find products to buy or sell in the supplying database or demanding database and can also register the product to buy or sell to promote worldwide business opportunities.

HINCO – possibility for cooperation

1. Representation

   We are searching for an associate – manufacturer, in the field of petrochemical and/or chemical production, who wants to sell his products on the Central and East European markets. We offer cooperation to firms that wish to tap new markets with their products in Slovenia, Hungary, Austria and on the Balkans, in the former Yugoslavia (Croatia, Bosnia and Herzegovina, Serbia, Montenegro and Macedonia). The cooperation can be of a representative form or as partnership in mutual investing or other forms. In Lendava it is possible to organize a distributive centre, where we can offer – storage and logistic facilities at your disposal, completion and/or production.

2. Joint Investment

- A renovated industrial hall of app. 1, 000 m2, warehouses of app. 1, 000 m2, premises of app. 5000 m² are at our disposal in the municipal equipped industrial zone in Lendava.
- We are searching for a business associate for investing in the production.
- We expect from the business associate to have a production program and a market for it.

Our part of the joint investment can be the above mentioned real estates and financial means. We are ready to take over the trading of the new product on the East and Central European markets where we have a well-developed business net within the HINCO GROUP.

Financial Information

Hinco d.o.o. Lendava is a customer of Nova Ljubljanska Banka d.d. Ljubljana, Slovenija.

Nova Ljubljanska Banka is confirmed as a first class European bank.

HINCO Lendava is confirmed as first-class bank customer, enjoying the most favourable loan terms and guarantees.

While we continue to be proud of our two-hundred-year tradition, we still carefully plan for the future. We are the major pasta producer in Slovenia, and our main activities comprise pasta production, bakery and milling.

Pleasures with healthy food

Our strategy is focused on the development of qualitative products for healthy and tasty food. We are constantly studying the lifestyle and habits of consumers. Our prime aim is to create quickly prepared meals protecting health and offering our customer a culinary delight. Quickly prepared healthy and tasty meals are the core of the modern dietary trend. Bio produced food is gaining increasing significance for the health conscious consumer. We are a company determined to keep the leading position in this field and to develop flavoursome, tasty and healthy meals adjusted to the modern way of life.

We trust in nature and therefore are committed to naturally produced ingredients. Our products contain no artificial colourings nor substances originating from genetically modified organisms. We operate according to the requirements of the ISO standard 9001: 2000 and the HACCP system.

www.mlinotest.com

Mlinotest d.d., Tovarniška cesta 14, 5270 Ajdovščina, Slovenia
e-mail: info@mlinotest.si

Perutnina Ptuj
1905

Perutnina Ptuj Group

Our Mission

We enrich the life of the modern family with the flavour of nature. Carefully balancing tradition, nature and state-of-the-art technology, we contribute to the better life of an individual, the local environment and society as a whole.

Our Vision

We shall be the leaders wherever natural flavour is appreciated. We attract with quality and friendliness. We are innovative creators of safe and healthy nutrition habits.

Along with the poultry production, which is our main activity we also develop pig farming, agriculture, wine production, feedingstuff manufacturing and a chain of our own restaurants.

Perutnina Ptuj has been active in the market since 1905 and currently holds a share of over 60% in the supply of poultry meat and meat products in the Slovene market. It is also market leader on former Yugoslav market and is continually present on Italian, UK, and Swedish markets and lately in Germany. It has obtained the international quality standards:

- ISO 9001
- ISO 14001
- HACCP

and meets the veterinary and sanitary standards set by the EU. Perutnina Ptuj is a proud holder of:

- EFSIS certificate
- BRC certificate
- HALAL certificate

and exclusive supplier for McDonald's in former Yugoslav countries. Perutnina Ptuj's production and processing of poultry meat are a fully integrated process. We ensure maximum level of:

- food quality
- food safety
- tracebility
- animal welfare

The taste of Nature

Our chicken are bred on small farms dispersed throughout the untouched natural environment of Slovenia.

All our products are 100% pure chicken meat, have a low fat content, improved nutrition value, a longer shelf life and GMO free.
We wish to give to modern life back what it lacks the most: a taste of nature.

With the expansion of our business network internationally and substantial investment in new technology, Perutnina Ptuj is becoming the leading supplier of ready-made chicken meat products in SE and Central Europe.

Chicken meat

Turkey meat

The excellent taste of our chicken and turkey is primarily the result of natural feed, which is mostly comprised of corn, soybean, minerals and vitamins.

Chicken products

The Poli sausage has been produced with the same recipe for almost three decades, and is preferred by consumers all around Europe.

Turkey products

Our range of turkey products is known for low fat content and low calorific value.

Convenience products

Our convenience products range is launched in modern packaging, available in boxes and 1kg bags.

Wines

We offer excellent wines from Ptuj's region.

Always there for you,
central to your needs ...

And why?

PBS.
POŠTNA BANKA SLOVENIJE, d.d.
Ul. Vita Kraigherja 5, 2000 Maribor, Slovenia
Tel.: +386 2 228 82 00, fax: +386 2 252 82 10

Because ...
we're one big family.

PBS.
POŠTNA BANKA SLOVENIJE, d.d.
Ul. Vita Kraigherja 5, 2000 Maribor, Slovenia
tel.: +386 2 228 82 00, fax: +386 2 228 82 10

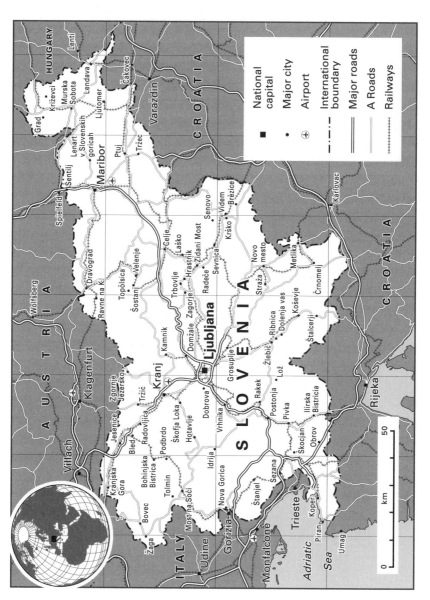

Map 1 Slovenia and its neighbours

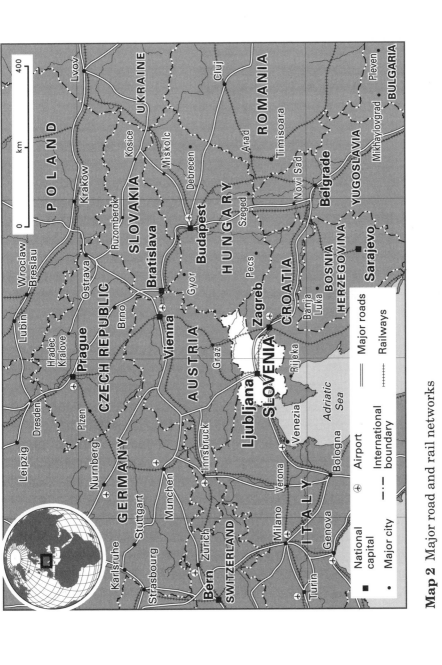

Map 2 Major road and rail networks

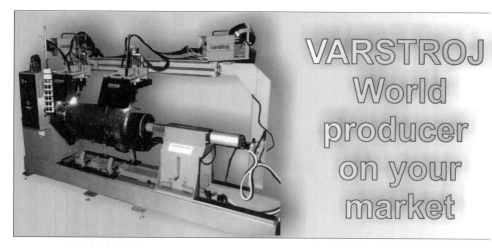

VARSTROJ
World
producer
on your
market

Štefan Kepe
General Manager

Varstroj is the leading producer of welding and cutting equipment in Slovenia. With own product development, orientation on foreign markets and always initiating ISO standards is aiming at Business Exellence Award.

History

The company Varstroj was legaly established on 1st January 1965. The company employed 70 people. First of all our production line consisted of producing the welding transformer Varex. In 1970 the welding equipment production exceeded to producing welding transfomers, resistance welding machines and flushbutt welding machines. The number of employees has already increased to 153. We would like to mention that soon after establishment, the company's activities exceeded regional and state borders in business way and tehnical co-operation with company Fronius from Austria. On 19th November 1994 the company went succesfull through privatisation process and it was transformed into a joint-stock company. In year 1998 we started working on Phare project named »Industrial success and competitiveness« and in years 1999 and 2002 we obtained ISO 9001 and ISO 9001:2000 standards.

R&D

Varstroj is investing a lot into internal R&D activities, education of staff and exploring of new potencial markets. In 1981 an independent R&D team was registered which has 7 listed members. Beside the permanent education in the field of inverter welding rectifiers (VARIN 1100, 1500, 1700, 2000) the company also developed a new synergic pulsed welding machine VPS 5000.

Varstroj aquired the ISO 9001 quality certificate in 1999 and ISO 9001:2000 in 2002.

Varstroj actively co-operate at different researching programs with faculties (FS Ljubljana, FS Maribor), institutions (ZAVAR Ljubljana, Technology center of Pomurje, Developing agency MURA Murska Sobota as well as with some ministries.

Our vision of development is in strategic alliances like partnership with other welding and cutting oriented companies like OTC-DAIHEN, Fronius and Kjellberg.

...already co-operate very ...ccesfully on the field of welding ...bots.

Sales

...e company's ability to react to ...urbulent situation in the market ...in other words, the company's ...lity to adapt changes is, first of ... the main indicator how strong ...e company really is. Varstroj ...owed this strength in the times ...Balkan crisis. Now we are ...ining back our marketing ...sition in former Yugoslavian ...untries and our trade mark is ...ite well known.

...r goal on the domestic and EU ...arket is to strenghten our brand ...cognition and increase our ...arket share. Varstroj wishes to ...ep the leading position in ...elding and cutting field in ...ovenia. In recent years we have developed increasing business in eastern and middle European markets.

We see the greatest potential market for our products in an enlarged EU, after Slovenia and other eastern European countries become full members. In last years we invested much efforts in order to regain marketing position on those markets which we lost due to democratic transformations in the 90's. Our export is also pointed to some Western European countries like Austria and Germany as well in some Eastern European countries like Poland, Czech Republic, Slovakia, Hungary, Romania.

We are also exporting to Indonesia and making our first steps on the markets in the United Kingdom and Australia.

There are many potential strategic markets like: Russia, China and Thailand.

Success

Implementing new technologies and introducing Varstroj trademark abroad will be the major activities in the future in order to remain a successful company not just on home market but also abroad. We would like to establish strategic links with our suppliers of material and machinery, especially by development of new products. With all strategicaly goals achieved we can quarantee our bussiness quality and find our place on the international markets.

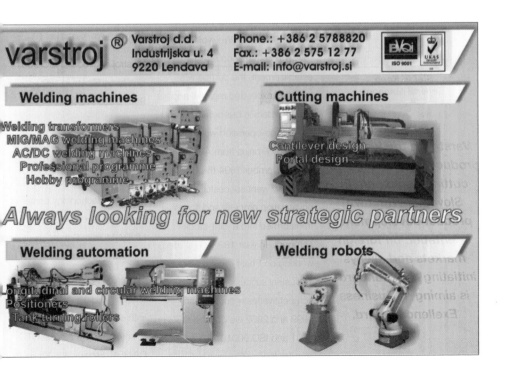

varstroj ®
Varstroj d.d.
Industrijska u. 4
9220 Lendava

Phone.: +386 2 5788820
Fax.: +386 2 575 12 77
E-mail: info@varstroj.si

ISO 9001 UKAS

Welding machines

Welding transformers
MIG/MAG welding machines
AC/DC welding machines
Professional programme
Hobby programme

Cutting machines

Cantilever design
Portal design

Always looking for new strategic partners

Welding automation

Longitudinal and circular welding machines
Positioners
Tank turning rollers

Welding robots

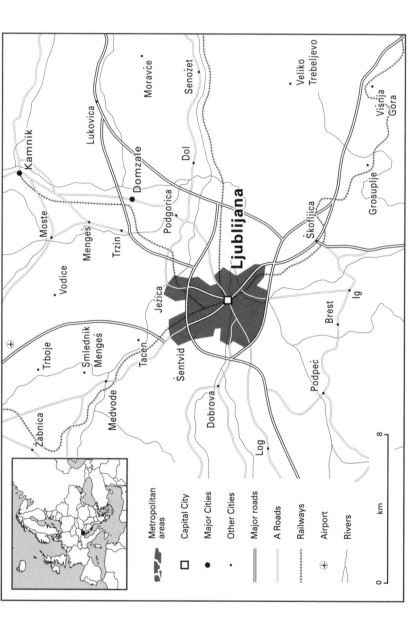

Map 3 Ljubljana and surrounding districts

Introduction

In her Foreword to this first edition of *Doing Business with Slovenia*, Minister Petrin affirms that the Republic of Slovenia is ready to play its part as a full member of the European Union (EU) from 1 May 2004. In many respects Slovenia is better prepared for EU integration than its larger Central and Eastern European (CEE) neighbours, having set its sights on membership from the early days of secession from the former Yugoslav Federation and, in the period of preparation for EU entry, focusing on the early adoption of as much as possible of the *acquis communautaire*. It also takes up its membership with an economy in sound condition and the prospect of gross domestic product (GDP) growth at the level of 3.5 per cent for 2004.

Secession itself presented many problems, of a political, economic and national security nature, which Slovenia has overcome in the intervening years since 1991. Except for Estonia, Slovenia has the lowest population, just under 2.0 million, among the eight CEE accession states, but this has not been a handicap in its achievement of a GDP per capita which exceeds that of all new member states other than Cyprus. Two ingredients in Slovenia's success have been the advantages derived from the formation of an independent government without an inherited communist-era bureaucracy and its inherited economic strength as the industrial and commercial hub of the old Yugoslav Federation. Slovenia has maintained good economic relations with its former partners and acts as a commercial conduit between them and the EU. From May 2004 this two-way traffic is expected to grow, bringing added value to Slovenia's membership of the EU25.

Doing Business with Slovenia is a new title in the Kogan Page series of *Global Market Briefings* which covers each of the 2004 EU accession states and countries further afield, including China and Russia. For foreign companies that are planning to engage in Slovenia, a working knowledge of the legal system, regulatory framework, taxation and audit and accountancy regimes is essential preparation for taking advantage of the opportunities for investment or market entry initiatives. A thorough understanding of general economic and business conditions and of key manufacturing and service industries in which a market entrant intends to do business is likewise important.

Part One provides overviews and commentary on Slovenia's political, economic and business environments. Part Two describes the legal structure and regulatory environment. Part Three is devoted to accountancy and audit, business taxation, the financial services industry and support facilities from the EU. Together, these three sections provide recommended reading for all those who have taken the decision in principle to engage and are moving on to evaluate ways and means.

In Part Four, some of the key industries and business services that make up the main sectors of opportunity in the Slovenian economy are described individually. The material is provided either by Slovenia's Centre for International Development and Cooperation or by expert practitioners in individual sectors.

We commend to you the input of all our contributors, who are themselves the sources of more detailed, authoritative information for those readers who find this book useful and are now actively planning their business entry into Slovenia. Their contact details and sources of further information are detailed in appendices.

Acknowledgements

Our principal knowledge partners who have provided most of the content for Parts One and Three are Bank Austria Creditanstalt, Deloitte & Touche, Coface and the Merchant International Group. All four Kogan Page collaborators have participated in the other Central and Eastern European titles in the series and will be providing a continuing flow of updates and material for the revision of these texts. Without their involvement, the book in this form would not have been possible and the contributions of individual authors are gratefully acknowledged.

The editor is particularly grateful to Pavle Pensa and Ozbej Merc of Jadek & Pensa, the leading Ljubljana law firm, for reviewing and editing the whole of Part Two. Our thanks are also due to the Slovenian Trade and Investment Promotion Agency (TIPO) for their consent to the use of content developed by and accredited to the agency and its associates.

Finally, we express our thanks to Minister Petrin for her foreword and to the Embassy of the Republic of Slovenia for their interest and encouragement in the development of the book.

Jonathan Reuvid
London

Part One

The Economy and the Business Environment

Political Overview

Biljana Radonjic, Senior Analyst, Civilitas Research

In 1992 Slovenia became the first of the constituent republics of the Federal Republic of Yugoslavia to secede. Since independence its socio-political landscape has been characterized by stability, continuity and consensus – features rather scarce in the wider region. This tiny alpine republic of fewer than 2 million inhabitants has achieved highly dynamic overall political and economic development, and has been ruled almost without interruption by stable and efficient multi-party coalition governments working in a technocratic manner and within a funda-mentally democratic political framework of a free press, regular and free elections and a good human rights record. It is generally considered to be the least corrupt of all the transition countries of Central and Eastern Europe.

In many ways, Slovenia represents a success story in the region of South-East Europe. In November 2002, it was invited to join NATO in 2004, the same year as it will also join the European Union. However, economic and diplomatic success appears to have produced a certain amount of complacency in Slovene society and there is very little support for remaining radical and painful, but nonetheless indispensable, socio-political and economic changes. This is perhaps most apparent with regard to reforming the financial sector and in pushing forward the privatization process.

The political structure

Under the 1991 Constitution, Slovenia is a democratic parliamentary republic. The Slovene parliament is a bicameral legislature composed of a 90-member National Assembly, elected to serve four-year terms, which takes the lead on virtually all legislative issues, and a 40-member State Council, elected for five-year terms, which has a principally advisory function representing various social, economic, trading, political and local interests. The government is led by a prime minister, elected by the assembly for a four-year period. The President of the Republic is directly elected for a maximum of two five-year terms and has mainly ceremonial powers, although he retains substantial moral authority. The Constitutional Court has the highest power of review of legislation to ensure its consistency with the Slovene constitution.

Political history of Slovenia before the break-up of Yugoslavia

Except for a short period of independence in the 7th century, Slovenia has had a long history of foreign domination, whether by the Frankish Empire, Bavarian dukes or the Republic of Venice. In the 14th century it fell under the Austro-Hungarian monarchy, and it is this period of rule, which lasted for six hundred years, that has had the most impact on the country and its people. The influence of German and Austrian cultures persists to the present day.

In 1918 Slovenia joined the Kingdom of Serbs, Croats and Slovenes, which changed its name to Yugoslavia after World War II. Within Yugoslavia, Slovenia was one of the smallest, but also one of the most prosperous, republics. Its local enterprises went the furthest in exploiting the freedom offered under the unique Yugoslav version of socialism and Slovenia was well known for its quality of goods and services as well as productivity, relying on the tradition of a fundamentally Western European work ethic. At the beginning of the 1980s, the Slovenes – just 8.3 per cent of Yugoslavia's total population at the time – produced approximately 18 per cent of the country's gross national product and one-third of all its exports.

However, even from early days, tensions existed between Slovenia and the rest of the Yugoslav republics. Nationalists within the poorer neighbouring republics of Yugoslavia played on wider public perceptions that Slovenia was economically exploiting the rest of Yugoslavia by acquiring cheap raw materials and semi-processed goods at below-market prices and selling the finished products back at above-market prices. Slovenia, in turn, perceived its financial contribution to Yugoslavia as excessive. The distinctive Slovene language and the distance from the federal capital, Belgrade, also made Slovenia more isolated from the rest of the communist federation than the other constituent republics, as did the fact that, from the 1960s onwards, Slovenia had the most liberal political regime.

As a result, Slovene politicians often tried to provoke a debate about fairer redistribution of power. During the late 1980s, the president of the Slovenian Communist League at the time, Milan Kucan, sought radical economic and political reforms within the framework of the

Yugoslav federation and Slovenia submitted ideas about reforms of federal structures, through confederation. However, these ideas were rejected by the federal authorities, especially the Serbian leadership. Further tensions came to the fore with a controversial trial, instigated by the Army against three journalists, including a nationalist politician, Janez Jansa, the current leader of the right-wing Social Democratic Party of Slovenia (SDS), which provoked massive demonstrations in Slovenia. Antagonism also arose following Serbia's decision to abolish the autonomy enjoyed by Kosovo, a move that was roundly criticized by Slovenians.

Breakaway from Yugoslavia and the war for independence

By 1989, the Slovene opposition was openly calling for national independence. While traditional nationalist forces had a role in this, the real momentum for independence was primarily based on the desire for political, economic and social emancipation, rather than territorial differentiation. This was particularly evident in the actions of 'Slovene spring', a social movement, which began to push more heavily for the formation of civil society groups and called for greater democratization, freedom of speech and a market economy.

In September 1989, the General Assembly of Slovenia adopted a constitutional amendment asserting Slovenia's right to secede from Yugoslavia and the first multi-party elections in the Yugoslav republic of Slovenia were organized in April 1990. These were won by the Democratic Opposition of Slovenia (DEMOS), a loose political movement of several non-communist opposition parties of both nationalistic and democratic orientation. Milan Kucan was elected president and Lojze Peterle, who still leads the Slovene Christian Democratic Party (SKD), was appointed as prime minister. The new government swiftly organized a referendum on independence, held on 23 December 1990, in which an overwhelming majority of 88.5 per cent of Slovenes voted to break away from Yugoslavia.

Slovenia declared independence on 25 June 1991, together with Croatia. An almost bloodless '10-day war' ensued in which a rather ill-equipped Slovenian militia succeeded in keeping the Federal Yugoslav Army within its bases and took control of the border crossings with little fighting. Since there were no territorial claims or ethnic minority issues involved, the Yugoslav government quickly agreed to a truce brokered by the European Community (EC) on 7 July. The war officially ended in the signing of the Brioni Declaration.

By late October, federal troops had withdrawn from Slovenia and on 23 December 1991 a new constitution was adopted that set in place the framework for a parliamentary democracy. After strong lobbying by Germany and Austria, the EU and the USA formally accepted Slovenia's independence in January 1992. Soon afterwards the country was admitted into the UN and the Organization for Security Cooperation in Europe (OSCE) and the following year it became a member of the Council of Europe, the IMF and the World Bank. Slovenia joined NATO's Partnership for Peace Program as soon as it was announced in 1994.

The first years in an independent Slovenia

Slovenia held its first presidential and parliamentary elections as an independent state in December 1992. Milan Kucan was elected president. However, in the parliamentary vote the Liberal Democratic Party (LDP), a left-of-centre party, won the most seats but was unable to secure a clear majority in the National Assembly. The prime minister, Janez Drnovsek, head of the LDP, formed a coalition government backed by a broad political alliance. In 1994, the LDP, factions of the Greens (ZS), the Democratic Party (DS) and the Socialist Party merged to form the Liberal Democracy of Slovenia (LDS), which has since remained the dominant party in Slovenia.

The first Slovene government dedicated most of its efforts to economic stabilization, a policy priority that was made easier to focus on given that Slovenia had experienced rather smooth political and social transformation, which, as Slovenes proudly claim, had already started as early as the 1970s. Still, being independent for the first time, Slovenia had to build from scratch its own army and police, a diplomatic service, monetary and customs systems, government institutions and administrative structures. All that was, however, achieved fairly quickly, as was the decentralization of power, initiated in 1994, when the pre-existing 62 municipalities were increased to 147. This figure has since increased further and today there are 182 municipalities plus 11 urban municipalities.

Although Slovenia never experienced the excessive war destruction and economic sanctions suffered by the other parts of the former Yugoslavia, nonetheless the conflicts in the region in the first half of the 1990s had a serious impact. Large numbers of refugees from Bosnia made their way to Slovenia. As was the case elsewhere in the region, the arrival of displaced persons created social problems and proved to be a source of antagonism among various groups in Slovene society. The Slovene National Party (SNS), a far-right nationalist group, led the agitation against refugees, accusing them of disturbing the labour market and increasing the number of criminal acts committed in Slovenia.

Slovenian politics until the present

Slovenia's second set of post-independence elections were held in November 1996 and resulted in another convincing win for Milan Kucan for the presidency. At the same time a new government came to power, made up of the LDS, the Slovenian People's Party (SLS) and the Democratic Party of Pensioners of Slovenia (DeSUS), which was again brought together under the premiership of Janez Drnovsek.

As expected, inter-party strife arose between the disparate elements that made up the LDS. Similarly, rivalry also existed between the centre-left LDS and the centre-right, rural-based SLS. This led to delays in adopting and passing legislation necessary for EU accession negotiations, which started in 1998, and the impediment of structural reforms, primarily privatization of large state companies and property restitution. The reforms were also slowed by the strong influence of former elites in both the LDS and the SLS, who competed for control of industry and public institutions. Finally, the presence in the coalition of the DeSUS, which defended the interests of the growing community of elderly people in Slovenia, made it virtually impossible to undertake urgently needed and radical reforms of Slovenia's pension and social security system, a process made necessary by Slovenia's low birth rate and ageing population. Although there was political consensus about the necessity to reform the pension system, differences existed regarding the role of the state in the new system and whether or not the system should be privatized. In particular, the DeSUS was against any reform that was based on a privatized system.

The government finally collapsed in April 2000, six months before its full mandate, when the SLS left the government coalition and merged with the opposition Christian Democrats (SKD). This left Mr Drnovsek without a majority and allowed the opposition to force through a no-confidence vote in parliament. However, the crisis, the biggest since Slovenian independence, was apparently resolved the following month, when a new centre-right government was formed by Prime Minister Andrej Bajuk, who is currently the leader of the opposition New Slovenia (NSi). But it was not to last long. Following scheduled parliamentary elections held in October that year, Mr Drnovsek returned to power at the helm of the current government, which is made up of a five-party coalition of the left-of-centre LDS and the United List of Social Democrats (ZLSD), together with the right-of-centre Slovenian People's Party (SLS + SKD) as well as the Democratic Party of Slovenian Pensioners (DeSUS). However, since December 2002 the prime minister has been Anton Rop, a former finance minister, who replaced Mr Drnovsek when the latter was elected to the presidency following the expiry of Mr Kucan's two terms in the post, the maximum permitted under the constitution.

General characteristics of Slovenian politics

Slovenia is characterized by political stability embedded in an advanced political culture based on consensus among parties of different political orientations. It is hard to tell whether the political consensus prevails in spite of the fact that all governments have been alliances of left and right parties, or precisely because of it. Consensus is probably a result of both long cohabitation between left and right parties in coalition governments and the fact that major parties do not blindly stick to their ideological standpoints. In any case, the left-leaning Liberal Democrats of Mr Drnovsek have relatively successfully formed strange alliances on both the left and right sides of the political spectrum in order to secure governance for more than a decade. What has definitely made matters easier is that there has been wide agreement on the country's overall policy goals. Most political parties have pursued similar policy objectives within what is, broadly speaking, a social-democrat model. Issues such as health care, the environment, education, social welfare and budget control are dominant in the public debates and Slovenes generally give greater emphasis to economic prosperity, good administration and rising living standards than to the adoption of purely ideological positions.

In many ways, such a high degree of consensus is unusual given the deep-seated personal rivalries among the country's leaders, most of which date back to communist times. Indeed, Slovenia's continuity with its communist past is very evident in post-independence politics, as many of those associated with the former Communist League of Slovenia managed to leverage the peaceful transition to independence to gain greatest political advantage. For example, Milan Kucan was an active member of the Slovenian League of Communists and was raised to the post of president of the League in 1986, before being elected president of the Yugoslav Republic of Slovenia in 1990 and becoming the first post-independence president. Likewise, Janez Drnovsek, the current president, served as a president of the collective presidency of former Yugoslavia from 1989 to 1990, and had his roots in the reformist wing of the party. Moreover, the rank and file of liberal democrats originally came from a reformed communist party and the communist youth movement. The absence of an ideological base to politics in the country is also remarkable given the high number of former communists in positions of power.

However, consensus in the Slovenian case also has its drawbacks. Although there are positive features arising from continuity and gradualism, the other side of the coin is that this often prevents radical changes where such changes are needed. While some post-communist states engaged in an elimination of former communist officials from politics, management of state companies and the police, Slovenia resisted antagonizing former communist leaders through conducting a systematic political cleansing process after independence. Besides their immense experience, strong senior leaders often use their political parties as mere means of support for their own political and business agendas. One therefore finds that strong factions are formed on the back of power-struggles between individuals, rather than parties, and this leads to rewards being given to key allies of party leaders. Consequently, transition is not being fully internalized, and economic reforms are sluggish as old elites with long-term vested interests still retain considerable power and influence, which has slowed down Slovenia's economic and political development.

This also means that a certain degree of latent corruption exists in the country, although it is by no means as prevalent as in other transition countries. In fact, Slovenia has the reputation of a comparatively 'pure' state so far as corruption is concerned. In 2002, the Corruption Perception Index produced by Transparency International, an international anti-corruption non-governmental organization, showed that Slovenia ranked 27 out of 102 states, with a 6.0 corruption index. However, the October 2002 report produced by the Open Society Institute (OSI) shows that corruption is more prevalent in Slovenia than outsiders generally assume, and these findings are endorsed by the business risk assessment of Chapter 1.6. The small size of the country and the practice of relying on personal connections in public institutions, which have long been interlinked with private sectors and media, contribute to corruption based on vested interests. The OSI report also claims that Slovenia has a poor anti-corruption strategy, inefficient anti-corruption mechanisms and defective legislation on conflict of interests. Also, there is a curious absence of public debate regarding corruption in Slovenia.

Likely future developments in Slovenia

The medium-term future of the political scene in Slovenia carries very few, if any, uncertainties. The current president of Slovenia, Janez Drnovsek, is likely to continue to wield considerable political influence behind the scenes despite his largely ceremonial presidential post. He still enjoys the permanent support of a large segment of the population and a strong majority in the government. The presence of various small parties carries the potential for future divisions within the governing coalition; however, these are unlikely to risk any serious economic or political instability. Also, Prime Minister Anton Rop, another LDS member, who is supported by a large majority in parliament, will lead the government smoothly until new parliamentary elections in 2004.

Looking further ahead, Slovenia will continue to maintain a strong, stable and consensual form of politics. With the passage of time, the influence of the current leaders will pass. This will help to eradicate the few bad elements of current politics in the country, such as corruption based on long-standing relationships, which has also helped to perpetuate the power of those who are opposed to making the radical reforms that are necessary in certain areas of the economy. However, and more importantly, the fundamentally balanced and steady political culture, which evolved as a result of the smooth transition period and continued during the first decade of independence, will continue to live on. Slovenia will almost certainly be one of the most politically stable countries in the expanded European Union.

1.2

The Economy and Economic Outlook

Jonathan Reuvid

With the lowest population except for Estonia (1.4 million) among the eight CEE states set to enter the EU in 2004, Slovenia benefits in many respects from the 'small is beautiful' syndrome. The gross value of its GDP at EUR 22 billion lags behind all but the Baltic States, but compares with that of Slovakia (EUR 25 billion) whose population is more than two-and-a-half times as great. Indeed, in terms of GDP per capita, absolute or adjusted for purchasing power parity, Slovenia's per head value of EUR 11,184 (EUR 16,841 adjusted) comfortably exceeds that of all other accession candidates except Cyprus.

Much of the benefit derives from Slovenia's inherited strength pre-secession from the former Yugoslavia, when it was the predominant industrial and commercial powerhouse of the confederacy. Although not untouched by the military and civil conflicts in other parts of the Yugoslav confederation, Slovenia has enjoyed steady and sustained economic development since 1991. Given this history, the unrealized economic potential for dynamic growth is less than in other CEE economies. Therefore, it is not surprising that GDP growth has tapered off since 1999 and has fallen below the 1995 to 2001 average of 4.1 per cent, as illustrated in the econometrics table of Chapter 1.6, in the face of a flagging world economy.

The economy in 2002

Some commentators' hopes for a more dynamic economy in 2002 were disappointed. However, an earlier Bank Austria Creditanstalt forecast of 2.8 per cent GDP growth was exceeded in the event when growth of 3.2 per cent was finally reported for the full year. In fact, the nature of Slovenia's economic growth changed in 2002. Foreign demand was surprisingly strong and increasing domestic demand, with personal consumption up 2 per cent and public sector demand up 2.7 per cent, also played its part. Investment rose by 3 per cent year over year after a decline in gross capital formation during 2001.

In 2002 the increase in private sector real wages averaged 2.3 per cent, against 1.1 per cent in the public sector, but labour market developments are curbing both wage increases and consumers' purchasing power. In 2002, while employment rose by a modest 0.2 per cent, the average jobless rate nationally remained unchanged at 11.6 per cent.

Nor was there any substantive indication of increasing consumer purchases on credit. Although credit extended to Slovenian households in 2002 increased by about 8 per cent nominal, the rise in real terms was only 0.5 per cent.

Consumer price inflation averaged 7.5 per cent in 2002 and was the highest among the EU 2004 entrants. Until recently, both the Slovenian government and the national bank failed to follow through firmly the undertaking given in 2002 to reduce inflation, which, at this level, is far from the Maastricht criterion for adopting the euro.

Current account surplus and FDI

No support is needed in 2003 from the central bank's national exchange rate policy as a result of the healthy growth of Slovenian exports in 2002. In spite of a decline in demand from the EU, the trade deficit was reduced to EUR 257 million from nearly EUR 600 million in 2001. A significant factor contributing to this improvement was Slovenia's successful export performance to the markets of South-East Europe. The trade balance also benefited from appreciation of the euro and the tolar against the US dollar during 2002.

A surplus in the balance of service transactions more than offset the trade deficit and generated a year-end current account balance of EUR 396 million, representing 1.7 per cent of GDP, the highest positive level achieved since 1994. Currency reserves were increased as a result of the surplus and were greatly boosted by the record net inflow of foreign direct investment of EUR 11.3 billion (analysed in Chapter 1.3). Import cover at the year end rose accordingly to 6.7 months.

Structure of Slovenia's economy

The structure of GDP by activity in terms of value added is detailed in Table 1.2.1. As in many EU economies, the services sector (60 per cent) contributes more than industry (31 per cent), with the construction sector (6 per cent) and agriculture (3 per cent) accounting for the balance.

The various processing industries, which account for 80 per cent of all exports, also contribute more than 25 per cent of GDP and employ approximately one-third of the active labour force. The disposition of

Table 1.2.1 Structure of GDP in 2001 – by activity

		%
A + B:	Agriculture, hunting, forestry and fisheries	3
C + E:	Mining, electricity, gas and water	4
D:	Manufacturing	27
F:	Construction	6
G:	Trade and motor vehicle repair	12
H:	Catering services, hotels and restaurants	3
I:	Transport, storage, communications	8
J:	Financial intermediation	4
K:	Real estate, rental, commercial premises	12
L:	Other services	21
	Total	100

Source: Statistical Office of the Republic of Slovenia, 2002

the labour force follows that of GDP, with 39 per cent employed in industry, 56 per cent in services and 5 per cent in agriculture. The revival in Slovenia's industrial production in recent years has generated growth throughout the economy, in which its adaptability is largely a function of its structure. As Table 1.2.2 shows, nearly 90 per cent of all enterprises are small and dynamic, and they make an increasing contribution to the economy.

Table 1.2.2 Structure of corporate sector in 2001

Size of enterprise	No. of enterprises	%	Total employed	%	Aggregate turnover (EURm)	%
Large	1,471	4.0	297,729	62.8	33,269	73.6
Medium	2,274	6.1	76,499	16.2	6,629	13.1
Small	33,445	89.9	99,217	21.0	6,780	13.3
Total	37,210	100.0	473,445	100.0	46,678	100.0

Source: Agency for Payments, 2001

At the other end of the scale, the largest companies in Slovenian trade and industry include:

Mercator	Trade
Petrol	Oil and petrol trade
Revoz	Renault
Gorenje	Household appliances
OMV-Istrabenz	Oil and petrol trade

Prevent	Seat covers, construction, etc.
ELES	Electricity supply
Telekom Slovenjie	Telecommunications
KRKA	Pharmaceutical products
LEK	Pharmaceutical products
Autocommerce	Trade
Slovenske Zelezarne	Steel production

Source: Companies and CCIS database, ranked by turnover (2001)

Within the manufacturing sector the relative contributions to value added in 2001 were estimated as:

	%
Food, beverages and tobacco	14.4
Chemicals	13.4
Metals and metal products	12.1
Electricity and optical equipment	11.9
Machinery and equipment	9.6
Textiles	8.3
Transport equipment	6.9
Paper and publishing	6.2
Other activities	17.2

Source: Main economic indicators: Slovenia, July 2002, SKEP GZS

Expectations for 2003 and 2004

Bank Austria Creditanstalt has lowered its GDP growth predictions for 2003 to 2.6 per cent, after growth for the first quarter slowed to 2.3 per cent, and for 2004 to 3.5 per cent, which is as much a reflection of external conditions as of expectations for the internal economy. This level of growth still exceeds the rates forecast for Poland and the Czech Republic in 2004.

The forecasts for 2003 are predicated on the following scenario:

● no global economic recovery;

● no significant improvement in the recessionary condition of the German economy;

● a moderate contribution only to growth from foreign demand;

● no dynamism before 2004 from domestic demand;

● with support from the public sector, a further marginal contribution only from gross fixed capital formation;

- a levelling off of the upturn in private consumption as a result of the more moderate growth in real wages.

Inflation and private consumption

In 2003, the uncomfortably high inflation highlighted above is being countered by a cautious budget and moderate hikes in regulated prices. Although the excise tax on tobacco has been increased to harmonize with that of the EU, tax on fuels has been lowered several times to prevent pump prices reflecting fully the hikes in international oil prices. As a result, the year-on-year monthly increase in the consumer price index in the first quarter of 2003 was well below the previous year at a rate of 6.4 per cent, supporting the revised Bank Austria Creditanstalt forecast of 5.8 per cent for the full year.

Of course, the expedient of subsidising pump prices is not a long-term solution because the reduced tax revenue puts a further strain on the public budget. Finance Minister Dusan Mrarmor has warned that revenue shortfalls of nearly EUR 100 million in the 2003 budget are expected. Bank Austria Creditanstalt predicts that the budget deficit will rise to about 1.5 per cent of GDP in 2003 instead of its previous estimate of about 1 per cent, but that, of course, presents no problem in terms of Maastricht criteria.

In mid-March 2003, the Slovenian central bank lowered all key interest rates by 75 basis points in anticipation of the lower rate of inflation working through. However, the government's monetary policy goal of a 5.3 per cent rise in consumer price inflation in December 2003 was retained.

By the end of the first quarter it had become apparent to the government that revenue forecasts had been over-optimistic and that a supplementary budget would be needed. On 22 May the government agreed the details and the supplementary budget was passed by parliament on 19 June 2003. Subsequently, the government and the employers have agreed to attempt to finalize a wages policy for the period 2004–05 as soon as possible.

At the end of March, the central bank stopped its swap-operation interventions on the foreign exchange market. The question has arisen whether the bank will depart from its unofficial crawling peg policy and attempt to keep the nominal exchange rate stable or whether it will allow market forces to determine the exchange rate. If the latter, Bank Austria Creditanstalt anticipates an appreciation of the Slovenian tolar (SIT) but would expect the central bank to intervene in order to counter strong currency appreciation. On balance, a stable trend in the SIT–EUR rate is expected for the balance of 2003. In this event, the inflation effect of prices on imported goods will be dampened and will facilitate achievement of a decline in inflation to the forecast rate of 5.8 per cent.

Predictions for 2004

The more favourable international economic climate foreshadowed for 2004 and increasing foreign demand are still expected to contribute towards the improved GDP growth of 3.5 per cent forecast for 2004. There are also two windfall elements which will help to bolster private consumption. Repayments are scheduled by then of most loans taken out in 1999 prior to the introduction of VAT; in addition, the initial funds yielded by the national housing savings scheme will become available in 2004.

The consumer price inflation index is expected to show a further reduction to 4.6 per cent in the yearly average and unemployment may shade slightly to 6.2 per cent. The budget deficit as a percentage of GDP is expected to hold at 1.5 per cent and the current account is forecast to remain in surplus at about EUR 150 million, representing 0.5 per cent of GDP. Import cover will be reduced slightly to 5.2 months.

With the net inflow of FDI forecast to remain at the EUR 670 million level, gross foreign debt should be contained at EUR 8,800 million, implying that its ratio to GDP should shrink further to 32.1 per cent. Under this scenario, Slovenia will take up EU membership in sound condition.

This chapter includes content derived from Bank Austria Creditanstalt Economics Department CEE-Report 3-2003 and Report 4-2003 and information drawn from publications of the Slovenian Trade and Investment Promotion Agency (TIPO) and the Chamber of Commerce and Industry of Slovenia.

1.3

Foreign Direct Investment

Jonathan Reuvid

Although the stock of foreign direct investment (FDI) rose steadily from 1995 when Slovenia gained independence to the end of 2001, other CEE countries, especially those which are already OECD members, have proved to be relatively more attractive to foreign investors. In an otherwise excellent economic performance, with GDP per capita exceeding that of all other CEE states, FDI seems under-represented.

By the end of 2001 the total FDI stock had reached approximately EUR 3.6 billion (approximately 17 per cent of GDP), but was boosted greatly by more than 50 per cent in 2002 with an exceptional net inflow of EUR 1,848 billion. Major contributions to FDI in 2001/2002 came from the privatization of Nova Ljubljanska Banka, the takeover of the Slovene mobile phone operator by Mobilkom Austria and the acquisition of the country's third largest bank, SKB, by Société Générale, France. The latter two deals together accounted for an FDI inflow of more than EUR 450 million. The forthcoming EU entry is stimulating FDI and inflows are expected to approach EUR 700 million in 2003 and 2004. The catch-up potential in FDI for Slovenia is substantial.

Inward investment policy

As a part of its preparation for EU entry, the Slovenian government has elaborated a comprehensive programme of measures to improve the competitive position of Slovenia as a location for foreign investments and to stimulate the further inflow of new investments to the country. Short-term measures include:

- increased accessibility of industrial infrastructure;

- employment incentives for foreign investment;

- increased free services to foreign investors provided by the Trade and Investment Promotion Office;

- systematic improvement of Slovenia's image as a location for FDI.

Foreign investors may benefit from a reduced corporate tax in free economic zones and a number of situations where foreign investors are entitled to refunds of social security contributions for new employment in such zones.

Slovenia enjoys one of the lowest rates of corporate tax on profits and dividends in the region. Foreign investors in Slovenia may reduce the taxable base for corporate tax by 40 per cent of the amount invested in tangible fixed assets (other than passenger cars) and long-term intangible assets. (See Chapter 3.3 for more detail on investors' tax incentives.)

Other good reasons for choosing Slovenia in particular as an investment location include:

- liberal foreign investment legislation;

- free and unrestricted transfer of profits abroad in foreign currency;

- stable political and economic environment;

- the highest credit rating among CEE countries;

- the highest consumer purchasing power among CEE countries;

- productive labour force and capable management;

- traditional industrial environment;

- established trade links with EU, EFTA and CEE markets;

- well-developed transport, communications and financial infrastructure at the crossroads of Europe;

- legislation and standards already harmonized with EU directives.

Foreign capital invested by country of origin

As Table 1.3.1 shows, Austria was the dominant source of FDI up to the end of 2001.

Together, the EU15 accounted for 83.4 per cent of total FDI. Only the Czech Republic among its fellow EU entrants is a significant source of investment. Slovenia is also an outward investor and its total outward FDI was USD 949 million against the total inward FDI recorded by Bank of Slovenia of USD 3,209 at the end of 2001.

Table 1.3.1 FDI in Slovenia by country of origin

	% at 31.12.01
Austria	47.6
France	12.0
Germany	11.0
Italy	6.3
Czech Republic	3.7
Netherlands	3.6
USA	3.0
United Kingdom	2.9
Switzerland	2.8
Other	7.1
Total	100.0

Source: Bank of Slovenia, 2002

Slovenian involvement in ventures abroad is mostly related to business activities in the other countries of the former Yugoslav confederacy and other states in transition.

FDI by sector

Total FDI at the end of 2001 is also analysed by industrial sector in Table 1.3.2.

Table 1.3.2 FDI in Slovenia by sectors

	% at 31.12.01
Financial services (including insurance)	28
Wholesale and commission sales	8
Chemicals industry	6
Pulp and paper industry	6
Manufacture of machinery and equipment	4
Manufacture from rubber and plastics	4
Post and telecommunications	4
Automotive industry	3
Other commercial activities	11
Other	26
Total	100

Source: Bank of Slovenia

Even before the foreign investment in Slovenian banks in 2002, the financial services sector had become the largest recipient of FDI, while overall foreign ownership had increased from the equivalent of 9.4 per cent of GDP at the end of 1995 to 17 per cent at the end of 2001. Investment in financial services remains dominant.

Data supplied by the Institute for Macroeconomic Analysis and Development shows that 4.3 per cent of all companies in Slovenia were in foreign ownership in the year 2000. The profile of these enterprises was that they held 13 per cent of all assets, employed 10 per cent of the working population, generated 20 per cent of aggregate operating profit and contributed 29.7 per cent to Slovenia's exports.

The largest foreign investors in manufacturing in Slovenia are identified in Table 1.3.3.

Table 1.3.3 Largest foreign investors in manufacturing (2002)

Company	Products	Investor
Revoz	Motor vehicles	Renault, France
Iskratel	Telecommunications	Siemens, Germany
Vipap	Pulp and paper	Ceskoslovenska obhodni Banka, Czech Republic
Danfoss Compressors	Compressors	Danfoss, Denmark
Tobacna Ljubljana	Tobacco products	Imperial Tobacco, UK
Julon	Synthetic fibres and polymers	Gruppo Bonazzi, Italy
Kolektor	Commutators	Kirkwood Industries, Germany
Henkel Slovenija	Cosmetics and toiletries	Henkel, Germany
Papirnica Vevce	Paper and paperboard	Brigl & Bergmeister, Austria
Sava Tires	Rubber tyres	Goodyear, USA

Source: TIPO – Slovenian Trade and Investment Promotion Agency, 2002

Regional distribution of FDI

The distribution of FDI among Slovenia's economic regions is very unbalanced, as detailed in Table 1.3.4. Up to the end of 2001, approximately 55 per cent of total FDI, representing more than EUR 4,000 per head, had flowed into the Osrednjeslovenska region around Ljubljana.

The average FDI per inhabitant for the whole country is about EUR 1,800, less than half that of Osrednjeslovenska, which is not only the largest but also the most economically advanced region, with low unemployment. In terms of FDI per head, Obalno-kraska ranks second, comprising the port of Koper and the holiday resorts on the Adriatic coast. With more than 100,000 inhabitants, this region benefits from an above average EUR 2,500 FDI per head. The most poorly invested

Table 1.3.4 Distribution of FDI by region

	% to 31.12.01
Osrednjeslovenska	55.2
Podravska	8.9
Gorenjska	7.9
Obalno-kraska	7.0
Dolenjska	6.3
Spodnjeposavska	4.6
Goriska	3.9
Savinjska	3.8
Koroska	1.2
Pomurska	0.7
Notranjsko-kraska	0.5
Zasavska	0.3

Source: Bank of Slovenia

region is Pomurska, located in the north-east of Slovenia at the Hungarian border, with FDI per head of no more than EUR 200.

Foreign investment parameters

Definition of FDI

The Slovenian Foreign Exchange Act defines foreign direct investments as all investments effected with the purpose of establishing permanent economic relations and effective control over management of a particular company or other legal entity through:

- establishment or capital increase of a wholly foreign-owned company;

- establishment of a branch;

- acquisition of existing companies that represent whole foreign ownership;

- investments intended for performing the activities of sole entrepreneurs (natural persons);

- more than 10 per cent capital participation or more than 10 per cent of voting rights in new or existing companies effected with the purpose of establishing permanent economic relations and effective management control; or

- loans involving repayment periods of 5 or more years with the purpose of establishing permanent economic relations, if the loans are considered as subordinate claims and if such loans were given to related companies.

Capital contribution requirements

Slovenian law does not specify a minimum or maximum percentage for foreign investments; hence, no ratio of domestic to foreign investment is prescribed and all combinations are possible.

The Companies Act specifies only the minimum founding capital for a company in absolute figures which is applicable to all companies, whether or not there is foreign participation. The Act also specifies the proportion of the founding capital that should be paid in at registration. At least one-third of the founding capital must be contributed in cash.

In the case of joint ventures, the domestic partner may make its capital contribution in: local currency (tolars), tangibles (movable and immovable property situated in Slovenia or elsewhere) and rights (eg rights to industrial property, including know-how in the form of intellectual property, securities, etc).

The foreign investor's contribution may also be in cash, in kind or in rights. The importation of goods as a foreign contribution to equity capital is unrestricted. A foreign investor may bring movable and immovable property into a joint company or into his/her wholly owned company. Cash contributions may be in foreign or local currency. A foreigner may also reinvest local currency derived from his/her share of the profits and of the remaining assets of a company that has been liquidated.

There are no special conditions impacting on the investment of rights by foreign partners other than those applicable to domestic investors.

The content for this chapter is derived from reports provided by TIPO – Slovenian Trade and Investment Promotion Agency, Bank Austria Creditanstalt Economics Department and the Slovenian Centre for International Cooperation and Development.

Foreign Trade

Jonathan Reuvid

The evolution of foreign trade since 1991

There has been a marked movement in Slovakia's foreign international trade away from the former COMECON markets towards those of present EU members, as in the other Central and Eastern European countries scheduled for EU accession in May 2004 and analysed in the Kogan Page *Global Market Briefings* series. However, Slovenia has stronger, traditional links to South-East Europe than its fellow EU entrants through its past history as an integral part of the former Yugoslavia. Thus Croatia and Bosnia are strong export partners and Bosnia a stronger import partner than Hungary and Poland. In 2001, 62.2 per cent of exports were to and 67.6 per cent of imports were from EU member states.

In Table 1.4.1 the evolution of exports and imports of merchandise and commercial services is charted for the period from 1992, the year of Slovenia's secession from the Federation of Yugoslavia, to 2001. During this period Slovenia's total exports increased by 42 per cent and total imports by 61 per cent. Except for 1992 and 1994, the total trade in imports exceeded total trade in exports each year, although a continuing surplus in commercial services has helped to contain the deficit within manageable bounds (USD 380 million in 2001). The trade gap in 2002 was EUR 257 million and it is currently forecast by Bank Austria Creditanstalt to rise to EUR 500 million in 2003, before falling back to EUR 300 million in 2004. This is hardly cause for concern, given that the trade deficit on current account was at the level of EUR 1,170 million in 1999 and 2000.

Thanks to a particularly strong net inflow of foreign direct investment (FDI), the current account deficit improved from a EUR 592 million deficit in 2000, representing 2.9 per cent of GDP, to a surplus of EUR 396 million at the end of 2002, representing 1.7 per cent of GDP. As anticipated FDI eases, the current account surplus is forecast to fall back to about EUR 100 million in 2003, before recovering to EUR 150 million in 2004, when it will represent a modest 0.5 per cent of GDP.

Table 1.4.1 Slovenia's exports and imports (1992–2001)

			USD million			
	Exports			Imports		
	Merchandise services	Commercial trade	Total	Merchandise services	Commercial trade	Total
1992	6,681	1,219	7,900	6,142	1,034	7,176
1993	6,063	1,391	7,454	6,529	1,010	7,539
1994	6,828	1,807	8,635	7,304	1,150	8,454
1995	8,316	2,016	10,332	9,492	1,434	10,926
1996	8,312	2,129	10,441	9,423	1,487	10,910
1997	8,372	2,042	10,414	9,357	1,404	10,761
1998	9,048	2,025	11,073	10,110	1,520	11,630
1999	8,604	1,896	10,500	9,952	1,519	11,471
2000	8,733	1,881	10,614	10,107	1,435	11,542
2001	9,251	1,943	11,194	10,144	1,430	11,574

Source: WTO international trade statistics, 2002

Slovenia's foreign trade partners

The shares of specific country partners, as revealed by the foreign trade statistics for 2001, are profiled in Table 1.4.2.

Table 1.4.2 Export and import shares of key trading partners (2001)

Export shares	%	Import shares	%
EU	62.2	EU	67.6
CEFTA	8.0	CEFTA	9.5
Germany	26.2	Germany	19.2
Italy	12.5	Italy	17.7
Croatia	8.6	France	10.6
Austria	7.5	Austria	8.3
France	6.8	Croatia	4.0
Bosnia	4.3	Hungary	3.1
Russia	3.0	USA	2.9
United Kingdom	2.8	Russia	2.8
Poland	2.6	United Kingdom	2.6
USA	2.6	Poland	1.4
Hungary	1.7	Bosnia	0.6
Macedonia	1.4	Macedonia	0.3
Others	20.0	Others	26.5

Source: Statistical Office of the Republic of Slovenia, 2002

Slovenia's most important trading partners are Germany and Italy, followed by Croatia, Austria and France. Hungary, the USA, Russia and the UK rank next among the top sources of imports, and Bosnia, Russia, the UK, Poland and the USA among top export destinations. The Czech Republic, Slovakia and the Baltic states are noticeable by their absence from the list of top 12 export destinations and import sources.

As in the case of Slovakia, there are serious implications for Slovenia's foreign trade, particularly exports, in a prolonged slowdown of the German economy, which accounts for more than a quarter of Slovenia's exports and almost one-fifth of imports. Although the majority of Slovenia's international trade is with the EU, exports to Slovenia from EU member states accounted for only 0.3 per cent of their combined export of manufactures in 2001.

Principal exports and imports

The main product groups of which Slovenia's international trade is composed are featured in Tables 1.4.3 and 1.4.4.

Table 1.4.3 Main product groups in Slovenia's exports (2001)

Product group	Value (US$ million)	% of total
Motor cars	727.5	7.9
Pharmaceuticals	431.5	4.7
Chairs and seats	418.8	4.5
Steel and steel products	275.8	3.0
Motor vehicle parts and accessories	218.0	2.4
Other furniture and accessories	200.4	2.2
Refrigeration and freezers	175.3	1.9
Electric water heaters	164.6	1.8
New pneumatic tyres	160.4	1.7
Paper and cardboard	146.3	1.6
Total	2,918.6	31.7

Source: Chamber of Commerce and Industry of Slovenia, 2002

In 2001, Slovenia's exports of manufactures totalled USD 7.78 billion and accounted for 84.1 per cent of total exports. Therefore, the 10 product groups detailed in Table 1.4.3 accounted for 37.5 per cent of the manufactures exported.

Similarly, Slovenia's import of manufactures at USD 8.28 billion accounted for 81.7 per cent of total imports in 2001, so the nine product

Table 1.4.4 Main product groups in Slovenia's imports (2001)

Product group	Value (US$ million)	% of total
Petroleum, bituminous mineral oils and derivatives	559.0	5.5
Steel and steel products	483.3	4.8
Motor cars	478.5	4.7
Motor vehicle parts and accessories	371.4	3.7
Pharmaceuticals	189.4	1.9
Petroleum gases and other gaseous hydrocarbons	176.4	1.7
Unwrought aluminium	170.6	1.7
Computer equipment	157.3	1.6
Commercial goods, vehicles	122.0	1.2
Total	2,707.9	26.8

Source: Chamber of Commerce and Industry of Slovenia, 2002

groups included in Table 1.4.4 represented 32.7 per cent of manufactured imports.

Leading exporters by key industries

The top exporters with export sales of more than USD 20 million, according to trade statistics for 2001, are listed in Table 1.4.5 by industry and product. These 26 exporters together accounted for 37.4 per cent of Slovenia's total exports.

Comparison of the detail of Tables 1.4.3 and 1.4.5 confirms how many of Slovenia's key export industries are dominated by this small number of major manufacturers. In a country whose population is less than 2.0 million, where 63 per cent of the corporate sector workforce of 298,000 is employed by large companies, perhaps this export industry structure is not surprising.

The five enterprises marked (F) in Table 1.4.5 have been the objects of substantial FDI. Renault's Revoz subsidiary, Slovenia's largest exporter, is the only automobile assembly operation in Slovenia and is supported by both imported and local component sources. Local vehicle parts and accessories manufacturers and Goodyear's Sava Tires subsidiary also make important export contributions.

In addition to the key exporters identified in Table 1.4.5, there are five major companies in the construction and building materials industry, SCT, Salonit, Vegrad, Bramac and Primorje Ajdovscina, which together contributed a further USD 23.7 million to Slovenia's exports in 2001.

Table 1.4.5 Slovenia's top exporters (2001)

	Export product	Export value (US$ mill.)
Metal processing		
Revoz	Cars	753.2 (F)
Unior Zrece	Manual tools, forged components	65.7
Trimo Trebnje	Roofing materials	36.9
Kovinplastika Loz		36.5
Tomos	Mopeds	25.8
Chemical, pharmaceutical and rubber		
Krka	Pharmaceuticals	224.8
Lek	Pharmaceuticals	219.5
Sava Tires	Tyres	159.8 (F)*
Cinkarna Celjie	Dyeing Pigments & Personal hygiene products	76.6
Henkel Slovenija	Detergents & personal hygiene products	59.3 (F)
Electronics and electrical appliances		
Gorenjie	Domestic appliances	541.2
Skupina Hidria	Electrical components (automotive industry & others)	103.6
Danfoss-Compressors	Compressors for refrigeration equipment	94.4 (F)
Iskra Avoetelektrika		93.2
Iskratel	Telecommunications	89.2 (F)
Agri-food industry		
Fructal	Non-alcoholic beverages	38.4
Pivovarna Lasko	Beer, non-alcoholic beverages	32.0
Ljubljianske Melekarne	Dairy products	27.4
Perutnina Pfuj	Poultry meat	20.8
Wood processing and furniture		
LIP Bled	Furniture	26.9
Inles	Joinery and carpentry products	22.3
Textiles, clothing and leather processing		
Mura	Fashions and ready-made clothing	62.6
Aquasava	Dyed textiles	51.4
Industrija Usnja Vrhnika	Leather goods	38.1
Planika	Footwear	32.3
Koto	Leather goods	27.2
Total export value		2,911.2

* data for 2000; (F) foreign-owned enterprises
Source: Gospodarski Vestnik – Financial and Business Database, 2002

The foreign trade regime and regulations

Free trade agreements

Slovenia is a founder member of the World Trade Organization and maintains existing commercial flows with its Central and Western European neighbours through membership of CEFTA and the free trade agreement with EFTA. It has also concluded free trade agreements with each of the following countries:

- EU member states;

- Baltic states;

- Croatia;

- Bosnia and Herzegovina;

- Macedonia;

- Israel;

- Turkey (not yet operational).

Non-customs duty barriers for countries that have not concluded free trade agreements with Slovenia are determined according to the GATT/WTO agreement.

Before the free trade agreements came into force, the average tariff rate in Slovenia's Customs Tariff was 10.7 per cent. The following is a summary of the tariff status under the listed free trade agreement.

European Union
From 1 January 2001, under the terms of its association agreement with the EU, Slovenia no longer applies customs duties on imports of industrial products of EU origin. For 2001, customs duty plus special import surcharges on agricultural products subject to quota were lowered to 50 per cent of the basic customs duty which was valid on 9 June 1996. The disbandment of the tariff regime will be complete on 1 May 2004 when Slovenia becomes a full EU member.

EFTA (Iceland, Liechtenstein, Norway, Switzerland)
All customs duties on imports of industrial goods from EFTA countries were abolished from 1 January 2001.

At the same time, concessions on agricultural products have been exchanged with individual EFTA countries under bilateral agreements providing up to 50 per cent reductions of customs duties within quotas for specific agricultural produce (eg coffee extract, tea essence, fish and fishery products).

CEFTA (Czech Republic, Slovakia, Poland, Hungary, Bulgaria, Romania)
All imports of industrial products, including motor cars, are free of customs duties.

All CEFTA member countries enjoy the same regime for the import of their agricultural products, except for a small number of products for which bilateral concessions were negotiated. Non-sensitive products are imported free of duty, less-sensitive products are liable to payment of customs duties at the same rates for each country without limitation and duties on sensitive agricultural products are paid within specific quotas.

Croatia
Trade in industrial products of Croatian origin was also totally liberalized from 1 January 2001. In determining origin, only the bilateral accumulation of origin is applied.

Annual bilateral concessions are determined for imports of agricultural products which are classified according to two lists: the import list and the export list. Duties are levied at 1 per cent on imports of agricultural products that are less sensitive to domestic producers and at rates ranging from 5 to 10 per cent on the remainder.

Macedonia, Bosnia and Herzegovina and the Baltic states
Imports of industrial products from all these countries have been free of customs duties since 1 January 1999.

According to free trade agreements with each of them, agricultural products are subject to customs duty reductions within quotas established separately for each year.

Israel
All imports of industrial products from Israel as the country of origin are duty free.

Agricultural products are traded on the basis of selective concessions according to established quotas. In eliminating customs duties and other equivalent measures, the principle of reciprocity will be applied.

The Agreement includes protective clauses in the case of major disturbances in national economies caused by its performance.

Free customs zones

Legal persons, singly or in concert, may establish free customs zones after obtaining government approval. The founders and other foreign legal persons and entrepreneurs may use free customs zones on a contractual basis.

Under the Customs Act, authorized legal persons operating in free customs zones are not liable to payment of customs duties, nor to other trade policy measures while goods are in bond and until they are released into free circulation.

Duties and rights of users

- Separate books of account must be kept for activities undertaken in free customs zones.

- Users may undertake business activities in a free customs zone on the basis of contracts with the founders.

- Users are free to import customs goods and domestic goods for export into free customs zones.

- Goods imported may remain for an indefinite period except for agricultural goods, for which there are time limits set by the government.

- Access, entry into and exit from free customs zones are under customs control.

- Founders and users must allow customs or other responsible authorities to perform their supervision.

- Users must keep records of goods imported, exported, consumed or altered in free customs zones for customs control purposes.

The Customs Act also allows for the establishment of less-regulated, open free customs zones.

Users may undertake the following activities in free customs zones, subject to prior notification to the authorities:

- production and service activities, including handicrafts,

- defined in the founding act or contract, and banking and other financial business transactions, property and personal insurance and reinsurance connected with the activities undertaken;

- wholesale transactions;

- retail sales, but only for other users of the zone and for use within the free customs zone.

Activities in free customs zones must not endanger health, life or the environment. Goods which leave a free customs zone may be taken to another part of the customs territory after payment of customs duties or re-exported from the territory.

Conformity to standards

Imported goods must conform to the general standards, technical standards and quality specifications applicable in the Republic of Slovenia. The import of goods requiring sanitary and health certificates and/or obligatory attestation must be accompanied by the proper documentation. There are special rules which apply to the import and transit of hazardous waste materials and other substances that pose a danger to life, health and/or the environment. Exports or imports of goods are effective on the day of assessment of duties payable.

Technical requirements

The Agreement on Technical Barriers in Trade (WTO/TBT) that binds WTO member states to ensure that international trade will not be impeded unnecessarily determines technical regulations in Slovenia. They are restrictive only to the extent necessary for the implementation of security, human, animal and vegetable health and life protection, environmental protection and the protection of consumers and other users and their property.

Technical regulations issued by Ministries for the protection of public interest in respect of individual products or groups of products must take into account international principles and liabilities arising from bilateral and multilateral agreements.

Only products in conformity with prescribed technical requirements and marked in accordance with relevant regulations may be put into circulation. Foreign documents on conformity are valid in Slovenia when they are issued according to international agreements concluded by Slovenia and in cases when foreign documents on conformity or conformity marking are equivalent to issued and established Slovenian technical regulations.

Product safety

According to the General Product Safety Act, products must contain all relevant information concerning the potential dangers that such products could represent.

Producers or suppliers must provide current information on the potential dangers of their products and, if necessary, remove products from sales outlets. Fines for infringement of the provisions of this Act range from SIT 2.5 to 10 million for legal persons and between SIT 2.5 and 5 million for sole proprietors (natural persons).

Standards

Slovenia's commitment as a member of the WTO to respect all liabilities arising from the WTO/TBT includes the Code on Standards and is reflected in the Slovenian Standardization Act, which is based on the same objectives and principles.

Slovenian national standards are drafted according to these principles and are abbreviated as SIST in Slovenian or foreign languages. Information on the adoption of SIST is published in the bulletin of the Slovenian Institute for Standards.

The use of SIST is voluntary except in rare circumstances where separate regulations provide for their compulsory use.

Slovenian Institute for Standards
The Slovenian Institute for Standards is a legal person with membership open to Slovenian citizens and legal persons established according to Slovenian law. The Institute has established relations with international standardization organizations (ISO, IEC, ITU) and European standards institutes (CENELEC, ETSI, BSI).

The Slovenian Institute is responsible for the following tasks:

- elaboration, adoption, publication and maintenance of Slovenian national standards;

- maintaining a register of Slovenian national standards;

- representing interests of Slovenian international standardization in international and European standards organizations;

- collecting, arranging and disseminating standards and other documents from this field;

- keeping databases on standards and circulating such information;

- publishing a review of adopted Slovenian standards;

- promotion of the use of Slovenian national standards.

Accreditation
Slovenian Accreditation is an independent national accreditation service that provides a transparent system of establishing the conformity of products and services. It is a full member of the European Cooperation for Accreditation (EA) which is the outcome of international mutual recognition agreements on accreditation documentation and the recognition of conformity documents issued by different accreditation bodies.

The Slovenian Accreditation assesses the qualifications of legal or natural persons according to the provisions of relevant national, European and international standards (series SIST E 45000, ISO/IEC Guidelines) and documents of European and international accreditation organizations (European Cooperation for Accreditation, International Laboratory Accreditation Cooperation and International Accreditation Forum).

Labelling and marking requirements

Labelling information must be written in the Slovenian language on the original package of products that are subject to quality control. The information must include net quantity/weight/volume details, ingredients, use and storage instructions and warnings important for the customer.

Rules on labelling in Slovenia depend very much on the kind of product concerned. As a general rule, goods must be accompanied by a declaration in Slovenian which includes the following data:

- producer (name, address, brand name);

- name and type of the product;

- measurements;

- date of production;

- materials or ingredients from which the product is made;

- water resistance;

- maintenance and cleaning (international symbols).

The labelling of foodstuffs, cosmetics, cleaning and similar products is subject to special rules.

The producer, contractor or importer (or agent in the case of consignment warehouse sales) must obtain certificates and comply with all requirements of the technical regulations before putting products into circulation. Durable consumer goods imported into Slovenia must be supplied with a written warranty, instructions for use and a list of authorized service agents, all in the Slovenian language.

Credit worthiness and payment transactions

The credit worthiness rating of Slovenia, well established by major internationally recognized firms in this field, is in the vanguard of all transition economies. The reform of Slovenia's banking system, introduction of VAT, harmonization of legislation with that of the EU, the sound monetary policy of the central bank and other relevant measures have combined to strengthen the financial discipline of payments resulting from foreign trade among Slovenian companies.

Irrevocable Letters of Credit (L/C) are still recommended for dealing with new customers. However, L/Cs are used for well under 50 per cent of transactions and more liberal methods now predominate in trade with established partners. Sight Draft (SD) and Open Account (OA) terms are in common use, with typical payment quotes of 60–90 days. Nevertheless, credit checks are strongly advised if dealing with newly established trading partners.

The overall collections experience is favourable and continues to improve generally. Foreign exchange/bank delays are generally less than a month, following rapid improvement of the banking system's infrastructure. However, there are continuing problems with company bad debts and inter-company payment areas, to which slow bankruptcy procedures contribute.

Content for the analysis of principal export products and exporters is derived from Slovenian Trade and Investment Promotion Agency (TIPO) material with TIPO's consent. Content for the foreign trade regime and creditworthiness sections is sourced from texts of the Centre for International Cooperation and Development.

1.5

Progress Report on EU Accession

Jonathan Reuvid

EU enlargement

The programme of EU enlargement under way at the start of the 21st century, and confirmed at the Copenhagen summit on 13 December 2002, is a major challenge for the European Union. There is an opportunity now for all the countries of the European continent to grow closer together by peaceful means by forming a political and economic union in which democratic rights are respected and the economy functions according to the principles of a market economy. The prospects of EU integration oblige the accession candidates to adopt a type of market economy arising from the tradition of Western Europe, not the tradition of the USA or Japan. This consolidation signifies a strengthening of the socio-economic ideals of the European continent.

The negotiation process which was launched in 1998 began with six countries and was later expanded to include six further countries. In December 2000 the European Commission announced that it expected the most advanced applicant countries, which included Slovenia, to finish negotiations by the end of 2002 and committed itself to make the EU ready for enlargement by the beginning of 2003. With the exception of Bulgaria and Romania, the process neared completion in December 2002 when the final negotiations were concluded at the EU Copenhagen summit meeting. The outcome was in doubt until the last minute, with final agreement between the Union and Poland, Hungary and the Czech Republic outstanding as Poland in particular pressed its case for the best possible deal. In the end the EUR 40.4 billion aid on offer to the admission candidates was supplemented by an additional EUR 1 billion cash for Poland's government budget in 2004–06, taken from its allocation for EU-financed regional aid, and an additional EUR 300 million for the other nine candidates.

Entry is now firmly set for May 2004, following a referendum about membership carried out in each country during 2003. The referendum in Slovenia was held on 23 March and resulted in a massive 90 per cent vote in favour of entry of all valid votes cast.

Slovenia's decision was never really in doubt, even before the spring 2003 referendum. From the beginning of its statehood, Slovenia has focused on integration into the international community as its principal economic and political priority and was foremost among EU accession candidates in adopting the chapters of the *acquis communautaire*. In March 2003, the first bi-monthly report of the EU commission in the run-up period to accession was published. Only Slovenia, among all accession candidates, was spared identification of any deficiency in fulfilling EC requirements and was commended for being on time with its entry preparations. Prior to the Commission's monitoring, the Slovenian government had amended the constitution to eliminate two legal barriers by removing restrictions on the free flow of capital and on the purchase of land and property by foreigners.

Although the government has made good progress in final preparations for membership, there is still work to be done in satisfying all the European Commission's requirements. For example, the June 2003 Commission report highlighted the long delays in court proceedings as a cause for concern.

In common with other new EU members, Slovenia is likely to gain some long-term benefits from the reform of the common agricultural policy (CAP), agreed by EU agricultural ministers on 26 June 2003. Of more immediate interest to Slovenian business are the opportunities to be derived from implementation of the CARDS programme, a special EU aid programme for reconstruction, development and stabilization of the Western Balkans. In this area of South-Eastern Europe, Slovenia holds an advantage over both current and new EU members through its geographical location and detailed knowledge of the local situation.

As Table 1.5.3 later in this chapter confirms, the Slovenian budget position is the soundest of all CEE accession countries. However, there is still a need to restructure expenditures in order to satisfy EU spending requirements and to achieve efficiency gains in the economy, and these considerations will be uppermost in the mind of the government, which comes up for re-election by November 2004.

The economic effects of enlargement

The new EU25 will have a population about one-fifth larger, with the new member states together accounting for just over 15 per cent of the total EU population. However, GDP will increase by about 5 per cent only, due to the wide income gap that still exists.

Table 1.5.1, based on 2001/2 data, demonstrates that, with a combined GDP of just over EUR 400 billion, the candidate countries will therefore account for a relatively modest share of only 4.5 per cent of the total economic power of the EU25.

Table 1.5.1 Comparison of EU15 with EU25

	EU15	New members[1]	EU25	Share of new members (%)
Population (mn)	381	75	456	16.4
GDP (EUR bn)	9,084	423	9,508	4.5
Real GDP (y/y in %)	0.8	2.3	0.9	0.1
GDP per capita (EUR)	23,856	5,661	20,870	−2,987
Unemployment (%)	7.9	12.9	8.1	0.2
Money supply M3 (EUR bn 2001)	7,087	250	7,337	3.4
Consumer prices (y/y %)	2.1	3.1	2.1	0.0
Public deficit (EUR bn)	164	23	187	12.6
Public deficit (as % GDP)	1.8	5.5	2.0	0.2
Public debt (EUR bn)	5,660	155	5,814	2.7
Public debt (as % GDP)	62	3	61	−1.1

Source: Bank Austria Creditanstalt
1) Estonia, Cyprus, Czech Republic, Hungary, Latvia, Lithuania, Malta, Poland, Slovakia, Slovenia

In reality, this disparity should be seen not as a problem, but as an advantage, and an opportunity with potential. Superficially, the new member states lag far behind the current EU15 average GDP per capita of EUR 24,000, with an average income of less than EUR 6,000 per year and inhabitant. In fact, all of them (except for Cyprus) rank below the least affluent country in the EU15, Portugal, with its annual average of EUR 12,500. However, once the lower price levels in the new member states are taken into account this income gap narrows from 1:4 to 1:2 in terms of purchasing power parity.

Aggregate comparisons represent only a part of reality and can be misleading. When the sometimes major differences in wealth within the various candidate countries are examined, the central regions of Slovakia and the Czech Republic, for example, are revealed as having a higher level of affluence than the EU average. For Slovenia as a whole, we have already noted in Chapter 1.1 that the national adjusted GDP per capita in 2002 was EUR 16,841, and this was second only to Cyprus among the new members and just over 70 per cent of the EU15 average.

The relatively small size of the new countries economically also reduces the possible risks to the stability of the new EU25. Accounting for less than 5 per cent of total GDP and only 3.5 per cent of the money supply, these countries would pose little danger to the EU25 as a whole even if they were to have substantially higher rates of inflation.

Moreover, the candidate countries have improved their stability in recent years; their aggregate inflation rate in 2002 at 3.1 per cent was only slightly above the EU15 average and several have individual rates of inflation that are lower. Nor is it likely that the uncomfortably higher unemployment of the new members, in particular Poland and Slovakia, will be exported to EU15 member states, since the shortages of employment opportunities in those countries are generally structural and not reflections of economic downturn.

Indeed, although restrictive budgeting measures in specific countries, such as Slovakia, may have certain dampening effects in the years ahead, the economic growth outlook in the CEE region is generally optimistic. EU accession will further stabilize the region and, above all, encourage investment in the accession countries, with all its positive stimuli for the economy of the region as a whole. The new member states seem likely to reach their potential for real growth of 3.5 to 4.0 per cent on entry to the EU in 2004, even without the support of a buoyant neighbouring German economy. Of course, the outlook does not preclude possible setbacks, as in Poland in 2001/2002, triggered by the global economic trend or the domestic business cycle. Nevertheless, factoring in the higher inflation anticipated in connection with the post-entry catching-up process and assuming stable exchange rate trends, annual GDP growth in euro among the new CEE members in the medium term could be nearly twice as high as in the old EU15. Their higher rate of growth would open up fresh economic opportunities which some EU15 member states, Austria and Germany in particular, will be well placed to exploit. Bank Austria Creditanstalt estimated recently that the growth will generate additional income of nearly EUR 250 billion for the old EU15 over the next 10 years.

A good indicator of which countries will benefit most may be found from the significance of their foreign trade with candidate countries. Based on this criterion, Austria and Germany are the clear winners, standing to profit most from the EU enlargement eastwards. Bank Austria Creditanstalt expects Germany to reap more than EUR 100 billion, almost half of the additional income over the next decade and equivalent to 5 per cent of current German GDP. However, Austria is expected to benefit the most proportionately, with the additional income of EUR 24 billion forecast over the next 10 years representing 10 per cent of its current GDP. On average, Austria holds a 5 per cent market share of the imports of the new EU countries, although nearly twice as much in Hungary and Slovenia. The German and Austrian shares of

Slovenia's imports are analysed in Chapter 1.4 as 19.2 per cent and 8.3 per cent respectively, with Italy and France accounting for 17.7 per cent and 10.6 per cent respectively.

The CEE economies compared

The relative economic outlook for Slovakia and the seven other CEE countries joining the EU in 2004 are compared in Table 1.5.2 in terms of major indicators.

Table 1.5.2 Comparative indicators of the CEE economies (y/y change in %)

	GDP real			Industrial output			Consumer prices			Unemployment		
	2002	2003	2004	2002	2003	2004	2002	2003	2004	2002	2003	2004
Slovenia	3.2	2.6	3.5	2.4	0.8	3.0	7.5	5.8	4.6	6.3	6.4	6.2
Czech Rep.	2.0	2.6	3.0	4.8	5.5	5.0	1.8	0.7	2.9	9.2	9.9	10.0
Hungary	3.3	3.0	3.5	2.6	4.5	7.0	5.3	4.8	4.3	5.8	6.0	5.8
Poland	1.4	2.5	3.1	1.4	7.0	6.8	1.9	0.8	2.7	17.8	17.9	17.6
Slovakia	4.4	3.7	3.2	6.6	5.5	6.0	3.3	8.4	5.0	17.8	15.4	15.2
Estonia	6.0	4.8	5.5	4.6	7.2	6.9	3.6	2.0	3.5	10.3	10.0	9.3
Latvia	6.1	5.5	5.8	5.8	6.2	6.5	1.9	2.9	3.2	12.4	11.8	11.2
Lithuania	6.7	6.1	6.2	7.5	6.0	7.0	0.3	0.7	1.5	13.8	11.5	10.5

Source: Bank Austria Creditanstalt CEE-Report 3-2003

GDP real growth prospects among the eight are not dissimilar, with Slovenia at the lower end of the scale. Increasing rates of growth are forecast for all the other CEE economies in 2003 and 2004, except for Lithuania and Slovakia. In Slovenia's case, GDP is forecast to fall off to 2.6 per cent in 2003, before bouncing back in 2004 to 3.5 per cent. These projections compare favourably with current year forecasts for the euro area and the UK of around 0.6 per cent and 1.7 per cent and of 1.8 per cent and 2.5 per cent respectively in 2004.

There is more uniformity in the growth of real industrial output. Except for Slovenia, all CEE countries are forecast to achieve output growth of 5.0 per cent or more in 2004. However, Slovenia's more modest 3.0 per cent forecast is above the 2.4 per cent level of 2002 and the sluggish 0.8 per cent predicted for 2003. Only in the Estonian and Lithuanian economies is 2004 growth expected to be somewhat lower than in 2002.

By 2004 consumer price inflation is expected to range from 1.5 per cent (Lithuania) and 2.7 per cent (Poland) to 5.0 per cent (Slovakia), with inflation falling back in Slovenia from a comparatively high 7.5 per cent in 2002, through 5.8 per cent in 2003, to 4.6 per cent in 2004. Generally, as a corollary of higher growth rates, less stability is forecast in inflation terms among the CEE countries than in the EU, where Consumer Price Index (CPI) rates of 1.8 per cent and 2.8 per cent in 2003 and 1.3 per cent and 2.4 per cent in 2004 are forecast currently for the euro area and the UK respectively.

Unemployment remains the weakest area of economic performance among all eight CEE countries, with marginal improvements only forecast in Poland, Slovenia, Estonia, Latvia and Lithuania and with unemployment in Hungary holding stubbornly at the rather lower rate of 5.8 per cent. Slovakia and Poland will continue to sustain the highest rates of unemployment in the EU25 for seemingly intractable reasons. Slovenia's unemployment rate is expected to coast downwards to 6.2 per cent in 2004, when it will be lower than in all the other seven countries except Hungary.

Foreign direct investment is analysed at length in Chapter 1.3 and Slovenia's foreign trade in Chapter 1.4. The two remaining indicators reviewed here are budget balances and gross foreign debt, each expressed as a percentage of GDP in Table 1.5.3.

Table 1.5.3 Budget balances and gross foreign debt among CEE economies (% GDP)

	Budget balance			Gross foreign debt		
	2002	2003	2004	2002	2003	2004
Slovenia	−3.0	−1.5	−1.5	40.4	37.3	32.1
Czech Republic	−6.7	−7.5	−6.5	37.6	33.3	32.0
Hungary	−9.5	−5.5	−4.5	55.2	58.3	58.0
Poland	−5.7	−5.7	−6.5	44.1	44.5	43.0
Slovakia	−7.2	−5.1	−4.1	55.7	47.5	43.3
Estonia	1.1	−0.3	−0.4	65.0	69.1	69.7
Latvia	−2.5	−3.0	−3.0	75.5	73.6	70.2
Lithuania	−1.2	−1.8	−2.9	411.4	41.4	40.8

Source: Bank Austria Creditanstalt CEE-Report 3-2003

All eight CEE accession countries maintain budget deficits, although Estonia's budget balance was positive for 2002. As a percentage of GDP the Czech Republic's deficit is forecast highest in 2003 at 7.5 per cent but is expected to decline to 6.5 per cent in 2004. Similarly, Slovakia expects to bring down its budget deficit from 7.2 per cent of GDP in 2002 to 4.1 per cent in 2004. In fact, all eight economies, except for the three Baltic states, are expected to bring down or hold their budget deficit to GDP ratios and, in Estonia's case, the increase is to only 0.4 per cent in 2004. Against the 2002 euro area budget deficit ratio of 2.2 per cent (UK 1.9 per cent), the deficit ratios of Slovakia, the Czech Republic, Poland and Hungary are currently high but are not untoward at this stage in their economic development. Slovenia's budget deficit ratio, forecast to contract to 1.5 per cent from 2003, is comfortably below the ratio of 2.3 per cent forecast for the eurozone in 2003.

Likewise, levels of gross foreign debt in the range of 32 per cent to 58 per cent of GDP should be comfortably manageable, remembering that significant additional funding is provided through EU budgets. Slovenia's gross foreign debt ratio, set to decline to 32.1 per cent in 2004, is bettered only by that of the Czech Republic at 32 per cent. Latvia's and Estonia's debt ratios are expected to remain worryingly high at the level of 70 per cent.

This chapter is based on content from Bank Austria Creditanstalt Economics Department CEE-Report 1-2003 and 3-2003 and East–West Report 4/2002.

Business Risk Assessment

Coface and MIG

Rating: A2

Default probability is still weak even in the case when one country's political and economic environment or the payment record of companies is not as good as A1-rated countries.

Assets

- Forthcoming integration into EU improves country's medium-term economic prospects.

- One of the region's most developed economies, with a stable macro-economic and political environment since the early 1990s.

- Ample foreign exchange reserves; foreign debt under control.

- Ethnically homogenous.

Weaknesses

- Industry dependent on the EU's economic situation.

- Number of reforms to be undertaken or stepped up (reduction of state interference in economy, equal treatment for local and foreign investors, greater flexibility of labour market).

- High unemployment.

Risk assessment

The country continued to enjoy moderate growth in 2002. Among the components of domestic demand, consumer spending trended lower. In 2003, the projected recovery in private consumption, together with export and investment growth, should lead to a slight pick-up in economic activity. The prospect of EU membership should notably boost business confidence.

Thanks to growing sales to the rest of Central and Eastern Europe, the country's external trade more or less weathered the slowdown in the eurozone in 2002. The current account deficit should, however, widen in 2003 because of the rise in imports driven by firmer domestic demand. But the country's external financial position should continue to improve on the back of broader cover by foreign direct investment of external financing needs as the privatization programme gathers pace.

Econometric data

Table 1.6.1 Econometric data

Change from previous year	1999	2000	2001	2002	2003 (forecast)	2004 (forecast)
In %						
GDP (real)	5.0	4.6	2.9	3.2	2.6	3.5
Industrial output (real)	−0.5	6.2	2.9	2.4	0.8	3.0
Gross fixed capital formation (real)	19.1	0.2	−0.8	3.1	4.5	5.0
Consumer prices (yearly average)	6.1	8.9	8.4	7.5	5.8	4.6
Unemployment (yearly average)	7.6	7.0	6.5	6.3	6.4	6.2
Budget balance (in % of GDP)	−0.6	−1.3	−1.3	−3.0	−1.5	−1.5
In EUR mn						
Merchandise exports	8,083	9,527	10,427	11,069	11,800	13,200
Merchandise imports	9,250	10,697	11,119	11,326	12,300	13,500
Current account	−655	−592	34	396	100	150
Current account (in % of GDP)	−3.5	−2.9	0.2	1.7	0.4	0.5
FDI (inflow, net)	64	144	414	1,848	690	670
Gross foreign debt (end of period)	5,147	6,726	7,497	9,300	9,100	8,800
Gross foreign debt (in % of GDP)	27.4	32.8	34.5	40.4	37.3	32.1
Import cover (in months)	3.3	3.4	4.6	6.7	5.8	5.2
Average exchange rate: SIT/EUR	193.6	205.0	217.2	226.0	233.9	233.0
Average Exchange rate: SIT/USD	181.8	222.7	243.3	242.7	209.2	189.4

Sources: WIIW, SNB, SORS, Bank Austria Creditanstalt Economics Department

MIG analysis

Introduction

The past two years have seen solid political progress towards the goal of EU accession, which remains popular. Regional rivalry with Croatia continues to simmer, with tit for tat disputes over the transport of oil products in 2003.

Table 1.6.2 Fourth Quarter 2002 Grey Area Dynamics™4: 39.5 (Europe and FSU GAD Rating: 60.87)

Fighting Index:	Low
Crime Levels:	Medium
Bureaucracy:	Medium
Cultural Integration:	Low to medium
Religious Extremism:	Low

Practice

Corruption and bribery
Under pressure from the EU, the government is making serious efforts to fight graft under a new Office for the Prevention of Corruption, with promising results. Ranked 27th in Transparency International's survey, the country is seen as less corrupt than existing EU members Greece and Italy. Despite this, problems remain, particularly in public procurement.

Regulation and judiciary
Problems in this sector remain a serious obstacle to efficient investment. Judicial independence is in place but significant backlogs continue to afflict the system, and piecemeal reform has not made significant headway. The system is undermanned and undertrained, and court procedures require simplification, but the judiciary itself continues to be suspicious of reform.

Organized crime
Slovenia's key geographical position makes it a transit point for organized criminal groups, most notably Albanians. Drugs, arms, people and automobiles are the key commodities, and Western Europe the key target. An estimated 2,000 women have been trafficked through Slovenia to the EU.

EU enlargement
Slovenia is set to join the EU in 2004, following the conclusion of negotiations in 2003. The accession process is not uncontroversial – farmers' groups continue to express vocally their dissatisfaction at proposed EU assistance levels – but majority support holds at around 62 per cent according to Eurobarometer. NATO accession is also due in 2004.

Essentials

Slovenia remains the most economically advanced of the six former Yugoslav republics, founded on a strong industrial base and well-established trading culture. As a result, alongside the Czech Republic, Hungary, Poland and Slovakia, it receives the bulk of the FDI haul among the EU candidate states.

The country's chief sources of inward investment are the larger EU states in general (the EU makes up 86 per cent of inward FDI), and Austria, Germany and France in particular. The greatest concentration of investments is in the manufacturing industry, where almost 38 per cent of all FDI goes. The financial services sector with 28 per cent is in second place, followed by trade and vehicle repair with 14 per cent. The sale of a stake in state bank Nova Ljubljanska Banka (NLB) accounted for the largest share of the FDI haul in 2002.

Slovenia's legal framework is considered advanced by the standards of its fellow EU candidates, and alignment with the EU 'acquis' is virtually complete in most areas. Ongoing telecommunications and banking privatization should ensure continued high FDI levels in the next year or two.

According to the Slovenian central bank, companies utilizing FDI in Slovenia are very important for the country. Although they represent a small share of the total number of companies, their size and success have generally been above average.

Concerns

The state's presence in the economy remains substantial, and privatization has been slow. Significant popular opposition exists, leading to continued frictions over the shape of privatization deals. For example, Italian Bank San Paolo SMI purchased a 62 per cent stake in Banka Koper early in 2002, but after long delays was limited to a 35 per cent share of voting rights at any AGM.

Despite strong trademark and patent laws, piracy and counterfeiting remain problematic, particularly in software and videos.

Part Two

The Legal Structure and Business Regulation

2.1

The Legal Framework

Jonathan Reuvid

Introduction

The Republic of Slovenia's legal system belongs to the same group as most of Continental Europe. The laws implementing regulations and other Acts have to be in accordance with the Constitution of Slovenia adopted on 23 December 1991. Constitutionality and legality are paramount.

The Constitutional Act was amended on 14 July 1997, 25 July 2000 and, most recently, on 7 March 2003.

The key characteristics of the Republic of Slovenia's legal system are:

● Judicial power is implemented by courts with general responsibilities and by specialized courts which deal with matters relating to specific legal areas.

● Founded in 1963, the Constitutional Court is the highest judicial body for the protection of constitutionality and legality. With the new Constitution of 1991 and the law on the Constitutional Court of 1994, it acquired a new role and function.

● The Courts with general jurisdiction are District Courts, Regional Courts, Higher Courts and the Supreme Court.

● Judges are elected by the National Assembly after a proposal by the 11-member Judicial Council. Judges are independent but are bound by the Constitution and the law.

● Under the Constitution, local government is carried out in municipalities and other local communities. The highest decision-making body in a municipality is the directly elected Municipal Council, of which the mayor, also directly elected, is the chief executive officer.

Structure

Slovenian law is based on the principle that no lower legal regulation can vary from a higher legal regulation. The Constitution is the highest legal regulation; this is followed by laws enacted by parliament and then legal regulations issued by the government, ministries and local authorities. This system, together with the rule that no regulation can be in conflict with an existing regulation, aims at consistency of the legal system. Legal regulations are essentially divided into public law, which regulates relationships between the state and its citizens, and private law, which regulates relationships between private persons.

Practice

District Courts are responsible for first-degree rulings involving criminal offences punishable by either financial penalty or custodial sentence of up to three years, as well as first-degree rulings in civil matters such as property disputes, civil disputes and probate issues. There are 44 District Courts; they also maintain land registers.

Regional Courts are responsible for first-degree rulings that are above the jurisdiction of District Courts, such as rulings on offences by minors, civil matters such as business disputes and matters related to forced settlements and bankruptcies. There are 11 Regional Courts; they also maintain a register of companies.

Higher Courts are responsible for second-degree rulings and decisions on appeals against the rulings of District and Regional Courts, as well as settling disputes between them regarding their jurisdiction. There are four Higher Courts.

The Supreme Court is, among other matters, responsible for first-degree rulings or decisions in some administrative and financial-administrative disputes, for decisions on revisions and appeals against the rulings of lower courts, and for settling disputes between lower courts regarding their jurisdiction. It also keeps a register of court practice in Slovenia's courts and ensures that it is uniform.

Specialized Courts   In addition to the courts with general jurisdiction, there are four labour courts and one social court which are responsible respectively for rulings on individual and collective labour-related disputes and on social disputes. For second-degree rulings the Higher Labour and Social Court is responsible. Finally, the administrative court is responsible for rulings or decisions in administrative disputes. For second-degree rulings the Supreme Court is responsible.

The Constitutional Court consists of nine judges, who are legal experts proposed by the President of the Republic and elected by the National Assembly, each for a single nine-year term. It is autonomous and independent and its rulings are binding. The Constitutional Court ensures that all laws and other legal regulations (which also have to be in line with all the laws) are in line with the Constitution, with ratified international agreements and with the general principles of international law.

It also rules on:

- constitutional appeals with regard to the violation of human rights and fundamental freedoms;

- disputes between the state and local communities as well as between different local communities, regarding their jurisdictions;

- disputes between courts and other state bodies regarding their jurisdictions;

- disputes between the National Assembly, the President of the Republic and the government regarding their jurisdictions;

- unconstitutional acts and actions of political parties.

Following a request from the president, the government or a third of the deputies in the National Assembly, the Constitutional Court gives an opinion on whether an international agreement in the process of ratification is in line with the Constitution. Its opinion is binding upon the National Assembly.

The Court of Audit is the highest body under the Constitution, controlling state accounts, the budget and the whole of public expenditure. The three supreme auditors (the president and the two vice-presidents) are elected by the National Assembly. The president of the Court of Audit can then nominate up to six other members of the Court of Audit.

The state prosecution service   Perpetrators of criminal and other punishable acts are prosecuted in a court of law by public prosecutors. They are appointed by the government and their function is permanent. The General Public Prosecutor is proposed by the government and appointed by the National Assembly for a term of six years with a possibility of a further term. There are 11 regional public prosecution offices and the Supreme Public Prosecution Office within which there is a special group focused on organized crime.

Essentials

The 1991 Constitution states that it 'is founded on the permanent and inalienable right of the Slovenian people to self-determination' and lays the foundation for the legal system, which is based on respect for human rights and the fundamental freedoms, on the principle of a legal and socially just state, on a parliamentary form of state authority and on the division of power into legislative, executive and judicial.

The Constitution can be changed following a proposal by 20 National Assembly deputies, by the government or by not less than 30,000 voters. Acceptance by the National Assembly requires a two-thirds majority of all deputies of the National Assembly. If 30 or more deputies so request, a proposal must be confirmed by the electorate at a referendum.

In Slovenia, the Human Rights Ombudsman has an autonomous and independent responsibility for the protection of human rights and fundamental freedoms in relation to state bodies, local administrative bodies and all those with public jurisdiction. The Ombudsman is proposed by the president and elected by the National Assembly for a period of six years.

Concerns

The current structure of the courts is regarded as too rigid and too expensive for the state. The June 2003 progress report of the European Commission highlighted the long delays in court proceedings as a cause for concern.

A solution proposed at the Justice Minister's third conference, which was mainly focused on transparency and trust in the Slovenian Judiciary, is to replace over time the combination of big and small courts by mid-sized courts which would operate more effectively.

2.2

Privatization and Denationalization

Jonathan Reuvid

Introduction

The first phase of the privatization process (so-called ownership transformation) in Slovenia is largely complete. The mechanism for handling the remaining unprivatized companies was established by the National Assembly under The Act on the Conclusion of Privatization of Legal Persons Owned by the Slovenian Development Company (1998), which supplements the previously adopted Privatization Act, Economic Public Services Act and Cooperatives Act.

After the first phase, the capital of all companies was distributed to various beneficiaries (among which a part was transferred to state and parastatal institutions) or purchasers. In the second phase, the state and parastatal institutions will sell their stakes to private persons. No general privatization programme for the second phase of privatization has been adopted. It is expected that at least partial privatization of those banks, insurance and telecom companies which are owned by the state or parastatal funds will be performed in the forthcoming year or two. The state also plans the privatization of those industrial companies that remained in its ownership.

The denationalization of property that was nationalized under the rulings on agrarian reform, nationalization, confiscation and the like is governed by the Denationalization Act and primarily takes the form of the in-kind restitution of property.

Structure

Privatization

Under the Conclusion of Privatization of Legal Persons Owned by the Slovenian Development Company Act companies which had not previously obtained the approval of the Privatization Agency became the property of the Slovenian Development Company in charge of selling securities and other assets of these companies. In 2003 the state has started with the liquidation of the Slovenian Development Company, in course of which all assets will be sold.

The Slovenian Development Company applied one or more of the following methods to achieve the privatization of those companies in its portfolio:

- transfer of 10 per cent of securities to the Slovenian Compensation Company and 10 per cent to the Pension Fund;

- sale of securities to authorized investment companies in charge of ownership certificates;

- internal distribution of shares to employees and former employees;

- internal buy-out;

- public tender, auction or offering; or

- privatization with simultaneous financial restructuring.

Denationalization

Although the preferred form of denationalization is the in-kind restitution of property, that is not always possible. In such cases denationalization is realized through compensation in the form of substitute property, securities (mainly bonds issued by the Slovenian Compensation Company) or money.

Beneficiaries of denationalization are individuals and legal persons whose property or that of their legal heirs was nationalized.

Practice

Privatization

The privatization process in Slovenia has been carried out using the following (one or a combination of) methods:

- sale of shares by public tender, auction or offering;

- transfer of shares to the Development Fund for sale;

- transfer of shares to the Slovenian Compensation Company and to the Pension Company;

- raising at least 10 per cent of additional private equity;

- sale of all assets (liquidation, sale by the Development Fund);

- internal buy-out;

- distribution of up to 20 per cent of shares to employees and former employees according to specific regulations and in exchange for ownership certificates.

The sale price of the assets of these companies is assessed by authorized valuers.

Denationalization

Those liable to return nationalized property are socially owned legal persons in the possession of such property. The property of legal persons in mixed ownership (social and private) can only be returned in the form of shares (equity participation).

Rightful claimants to the property of socially owned companies can request a share of the company under conditions stipulated by law. The enterprise as a whole may also be restituted to the rightful claimant.

A specific methodology has been issued by the Ministry of Finance for assessing the market value of nationalized property according to its state at the time of its nationalization. Claims for the denationalization of nationalized enterprises are decided by the relevant municipal administrative body.

Essentials

Early in the privatization process the government issued ownership certificates to all Slovenian citizens, which were either exchanged for shares of the company in which the holder is or was employed, or used in the purchase of shares of investment funds which used the certificates to build a portfolio of shares of companies of their choice.

Concerns

In denationalization cases, property cannot be returned if ownership rights are held by natural or private legal persons. Personal property cannot in general be returned. The denationalization process is slow and 10 years after the law came into force, around 30 per cent of cases remain unsolved.

Public opinion is not in favour of privatization and opposes the selling of state ownership to foreign investors. Such sentiments are slowing down the process of the second phase of privatization.

2.3

Alternative Corporate Structures

Jonathan Reuvid

Introduction

Foreign legal entities and foreigners may establish business operations in Slovenia in a variety of authorized legal forms. According to the Foreign Exchange Act, all investments effected with the purpose of establishing permanent economic relations and effective control over management of a particular company or other legal entity are classified as foreign direct investment (FDI).

Structure

The following are the alternative organizational forms:

- **General partnership (d.n.o.):** unlimited liability; no founding capital; founded by agreement between at least two founders.

- **Limited partnership (k.d.):** general partners have unlimited liability; limited partners have limited liability; founded by agreement between at least two founders of which at least one must have unlimited and at least one limited liability.

- **Joint stock company (d.d.):** minimum founding capital of SIT 6 million and one founder, 1/3 of which must be contributed in cash; limited liability.

- **Limited liability company (d.o.o.):** minimum founding capital of SIT 2.1 million, one-third of which must be contributed in cash; minimum 1 and maximum 50 shareholders; contributions in kind must be fully paid in before registration; limited liability.

- **Limited partnership by shares (k.d.d.):** at least one partner has unlimited liability; limited partners not liable for company obligations; may issue shares; articles of association must be adopted by at least five persons.

Alternatively, foreign companies which have been registered in their country of origin for at least two years may establish branches in Slovenia. Representative offices of foreign companies must be organized as branches. Representative offices of foreign banks are regulated by the Banking Act.

Practice

General partnership

General partnerships are legal persons who obtain such status by court registration after signing an act on establishment. A partner may be a domestic or foreign legal or natural person. The partnership name must contain the name of at least one partner and the abbreviation d.n.o.

Partners may contribute in cash or kind as well as in rights or services. No contributions are required for the establishment of the partnership. Unless the act of establishment provides otherwise, all partners must participate in the management of the partnership. Partners cannot dispose of their share freely without consent of the other partner(s).

Limited partnership

Partners may have domestic or foreign legal or natural status where at least one general partner is fully liable (including private assets) and at least one is not liable for the partnership's obligations. Limited partners may contribute to the partnership in cash, kind, property rights and/or services. General partners are subject to the same provisions that govern general partnerships. Legal relations between the partners are regulated by contract. Limited partners are not allowed to take part in management of the company, or they become liable as are the general partners.

The name of the limited partnership must contain the name of at least one general partner and the abbreviation k.d. The name of the limited partnership may not contain the names of limited partners.

Joint stock company

The minimum single founder/shareholder may be a natural or legal, foreign or domestic person. At least one-third of the shares must be paid in in cash. Before registration at least 25 per cent of the nominal value of shares payable in cash must be paid in, unless there is only one founder – then the whole value of shares issued must be paid in prior to registration or proper security must be offered. Assessment by a certified independent accountant is required if the company was founded by contributions in kind.

Shares can be bearer shares or registered shares and must be denominated in multiples of SIT 1,000 with a minimum face value of SIT 1,000. Registered shares must be issued if the notional value has not been fully paid up. Preference shares may be issued up to a maximum of 50 per cent of the capital of the company. Multiple-vote shares are not permitted.

The management board (minimum one member) is elected by the supervisory board for a renewable period of a maximum of five years. If there is no supervisory board, the management must have at least three members. The articles of association may provide for the management to participate in profits. A supervisory board is mandatory for companies with more than SIT 410 million of founding capital, or more than 500 employees, or more than 100 shareholders, or listed on the stock exchange, or founded successively. A supervisory board is also mandatory for banks, insurance companies and investment companies.

Limited liability company

If a limited liability company has more than 50 shareholders, approval by the minister responsible for economic affairs must be obtained.

The minimum contribution of each shareholder to the minimum founding capital of SIT 2.1 million is SIT 14,000. At least one-third of the founding capital must be paid in in cash. Before registration, at least 25 per cent of each shareholder's cash contribution must be paid in. The sum of all paid contributions must be at least SIT 1.1 million. Where the value of contributions in kind exceeds SIT 14 million, their value must be assessed by a certified independent accountant.

Management rights of shareholders are provided by the agreement of incorporation or, in the absence of such provisions, the shareholders' authority is defined by the Companies Act. Normally, each shareholder has one vote for each SIT 14,000 of his or her contribution at shareholders' meetings unless the agreement of incorporation provides otherwise.

Limited partnership by shares

One or several partners, called general partners, assume full liability besides the corporation itself. The general partners are entrusted with the right of management, of which, as in the case of any kind of limited partnership, they may be deprived only by court order.

Legal relationships between the general partners and shareholders are regulated by the same provisions as for limited partnerships. Other aspects of organization and business structure are governed by the provisions regulating joint stock companies.

The limited partnership by shares may be established by at least five founders who adopt the company's articles of association.

Branches

A branch performs its business activities in the name and on behalf of the parent company. The name and address of the parent company must be used in business transactions. The parent company is liable for all the obligations of the branch.

The branch must be registered with the competent court in Slovenia. All documents must be filed in the original language and accompanied by an official translation into the Slovenian language.

Since 1 February 1999, branches of EU member countries' companies established in Slovenia have been granted full national treatment.

Essentials

A foreigner may set up whatever legally recognized form of a company based on the Companies Act it considers most appropriate. All forms of company, except for silent partnerships, acquire the character of a legal entity by being entered into the court register. Before registration many formalities have to be completed for which legal advice and guidance are recommended.

A foreign person may be an exclusive or partial owner. A company founded in this way enjoys, legally, on the territory of the Republic of Slovenia, the same rights, obligations and responsibilities as the companies with a parent board office in Slovenia. Therefore, a status of domestic legal entity is acquired. The owner is free to transfer capital abroad, after all taxes and contributions have been paid.

In addition to founding an individual company, foreigners can invest in existing companies. In companies where equity shares are not securities (partnerships and limited liability companies), investments will be performed in agreement with the company's partners and by joining the partnership agreement.

Concerns

Limited partners in a limited partnership are excluded from the right of management and representation and may not oppose business decisions of the partnership. However, by agreement with a general partner, a limited partner may act as a proxy.

2.4

Foreign Investor Operations

Jonathan Reuvid

Introduction

There are a number of regulations relating to the conduct of foreign-owned businesses and their financial and operational management of which investors should be aware when planning to set up in business or investing in Slovenia. Overviews of the essentials on the following topics are given in this chapter:

- rights of foreigners doing business in Slovenia;

- capital contribution requirements;

- contractual joint ventures;

- takeovers;

- financial operations;

- performance of economic activities abroad;

- dispute resolution; and

- bankruptcy and liquidation.

Slovenia is a member of, and adheres to, all recognized international conventions relating to the treatment of intellectual property and its legislation is in line with these conventions.

Rights of foreigners doing business in Slovenia

Foreign investments in any form enjoy full national treatment. Companies with foreign capital participation and wholly foreign-owned companies registered in Slovenia (including EU branches) have the status of resident Slovenian legal entities established and operating in accordance with Slovenian regulations.

Companies with foreign capital participation have the same rights and obligations as other Slovenian companies in terms of ownership (including real estate), imports, exports, customs duties, taxation, etc.

Foreign exchange transactions

According to the Foreign Exchange Act (1999), foreign investments enjoy the following rights:

- Suitable compensation in kind and in cash is paid in the event of expropriation or other government measures if the principle of reciprocity is established.

- Foreign investment contracts concluded on the basis of the former Foreign Investment Act (replaced by the Foreign Exchange Act) are implemented fully according to the original contract until expiry.

- Long-term contracts registered up to enforcement of the Foreign Exchange Act are implemented according to such contracts until their expiry.

- Profits, purchase money in the case of assets sold and the remaining assets or capital transaction after the liquidation of companies are freely transferable after settlement of outstanding tax liabilities. Resident legal persons (apart from banks) and non-resident persons may acquire foreign exchange only from authorized commercial banks. Resident natural persons may acquire foreign exchange from authorized banks and exchange offices. In case of foreign currency transactions between resident legal persons, resident sole proprietors and branches of foreign legal persons on the one hand and non-residents on the other, foreign currency must in general immediately be deposited with a commercial bank.

Admissibility (restrictions to certain activities)

All sectors of the economy are open to foreign investors. Prohibitions on any foreign direct investment (FDI) apply only in the fields of military equipment and obligatory pension and health insurance financed from the budget.

Capital contribution requirements

The law does not specify a minimum or maximum percentage for foreign investments. Therefore, no ratio of domestic to foreign investment is prescribed and all combinations are possible except in the specific sectors listed above.

The Companies Act specifies only the minimum founding capital for a company in absolute figures, which is applicable to all companies, whether there is a foreign participation or not. It also specifies the proportion of the founding capital that should be paid in at registration (see Chapter 2.3). At least one-third of the founding capital must be contributed in cash.

The domestic partner may contribute local currency (tolars), tangibles (movable and immovable property located in Slovenia or in other countries) and rights (eg to industrial property, including know-how in the form of intellectual property, securities, etc).

The foreign investors' capital contribution may also be in cash, in rights or in kind. A foreign investor may bring movable and immovable property into a joint company or into a wholly owned company. Cash contributions may be in a foreign currency or in local currency. A foreigner may also reinvest local currency deriving from his or her share of the profits of another company and of the remaining assets of a company that has been liquidated.

There are no special conditions other than those applicable to domestic investors that impact on the investment of rights by foreign partners.

Contractual joint ventures

Contractual joint ventures that were available according to provisions of the former Foreign Investment Act are no longer admissible, owing to the adoption of the new Foreign Exchange Act which is elaborated according to European Union Standards which have replaced the Foreign Investment Act. Contractual joint ventures are, however, still possible but they do fall under the restrictions of the Foreign Exchange Act.

Takeovers

The Takeovers Act regulates the modalities and conditions for acquiring publicly traded shares issued by joint-stock companies, when legal or natural persons acquire a 25 per cent share of the voting rights of a company. The main purpose of this Act is to protect investors participating in the securities market and minority shareholders of companies where the transfer of a controlling stake occurs. The Act is based on the provisions of the draft European Directive on Takeovers No. 13:

- equal treatment of all shareholders;

- mandatory bid for takeover when the controlling share reaches the threshold of 25 per cent of voting rights;

- obligatory publication of relevant data; and
- reduction of defence mechanisms which would impede a takeover.

Foreign acquisitions

The Takeovers Act provides for the equal treatment of foreign and domestic investors. Foreign investors (foreign legal and natural persons) may acquire securities of joint-stock companies on the stock exchange or on the over-the-counter market and perform takeover activities subject to the same conditions as domestic investors.

Administrative control

Based on proposals of the Ministry for Economy, the Slovenian government issues permits for acquisitions of more than a 25 per cent share of privatized companies with capital exceeding SIT 800 million in the first five years of registration of privatization.

An investor wishing to make a takeover bid in a company must immediately notify his or her intention to the Securities Market Commission, the Office of Protection of Competition and the management of the target company.

The Securities Market Commission issues permits for acquiring a controlling share if the bidding process contains all data prescribed by law, if the bid is drafted according to the Takeovers Act and if financial resources for carrying out the bid are secured through a cash deposit or a first-rank bank guarantee.

Financial operations of companies

The Financial Operations of Companies Act provides that all companies, other than banks, insurance companies, broking companies and management companies, must perform their business operations in such manner that they are at any time capable of fulfilling their liabilities, when due, in a timely and permanent manner.

Companies are by law removed from the court register when either of the following conditions is fulfilled: the company has not presented its annual reports to the organization responsible for disclosure of such information for two consecutive business years, or the company has no assets (automatically fulfilled if the company is not effecting payments through its registered account for the period of 12 months).

Members of the management and supervisory boards and shareholders or partners are liable to pay damages incurred by creditors for the infringement of provisions of the Financial Operations of Companies Act. Their liability is limited to specific amounts stipulated by the Financial Operations of Companies Act.

Performance of economic activities abroad

Residents, as defined by the Foreign Exchange Act, must within 30 days of concluding a capital transaction abroad (including all subsequent amendments) inscribe the details of the investment into the register of direct investments abroad maintained by the Ministry of Finance.

Dispute resolution

Recognition and enforcement of foreign arbitration awards

Foreign arbitration awards are recognized in Slovenia when the requesting party appends to its application to the competent court:

- the original or a certified copy of the arbitration award;

- the original or a certified copy of the arbitration contract;

- a certified translation into the official language of the Slovenian court.

Recognition and enforcement of foreign arbitration awards are rejected in cases where:

- the contents of the award cannot be subject to arbitration according to Slovenian law;

- the effect of the recognition and enforcement is contrary to public order;

- no reciprocity is established;

- the arbitration contract is not concluded in writing;

- one of the parties was not legally capable of concluding the arbitration contract;

- the arbitration contract is invalid according to the designated law, or if no law was designated, according to the law of the country in which it was issued;

- the addressed party was not properly informed on the appointment of arbitrators or on the arbitration procedure or was otherwise impeded in asserting its rights;

- the composition of the arbitration court or the arbitration procedure was not in accordance with the arbitration contract;

- the arbitration court exceeded its authority under the arbitration contract;

- the award is not final and enforceable or its enforcement has been suspended by the proper authorities of the country in which the award was issued or the proper authorities of the country under the laws of which it was issued;

- the verdict of the award is in contradiction or incomprehensible.

If a Slovenian court establishes that there are no obstacles to the recognition and enforcement of the foreign arbitration award, it issues an enforcement decision against which an appeal may be lodged within 15 days.

Permanent arbitration court

Slovenia has ratified the New York Convention on the Recognition and Enforcement of Foreign Arbitration Awards and has successively adopted the European Convention in International Commercial Arbitration and the Washington Convention on the Settlement of Investment Disputes Between States and Nationals of Other States.

The permanent Court of Arbitration, attached to the Slovenian Chamber of Commerce and Industry, is the only permanent Slovenian court of arbitration which can settle disputes arising out of domestic and international contracts.

Bankruptcy and liquidation

The focus of bankruptcy proceedings in the Republic of Slovenia is on the potential for the financial reorganization of a company in compulsory settlement proceedings. This provision enables the implementation of statutory reorganization, rationalization of business activities, and the establishment of sound capital links with other companies (including the dismissal of surplus workers).

The definition of debtors includes independent entrepreneurs, commercial companies, cooperatives, public companies and other legal and natural persons determined by special acts. The following conditions apply to bankruptcy proceedings against debtors:

- Bankruptcy proceedings are initiated against those debtors with a long history of insolvency or being heavily encumbered by debts.

- Bankruptcy proceedings cannot be initiated against debtors with only one creditor, and bankruptcy procedures against debtors whose property value is insufficient to cover the cost of the proceedings are initiated and immediately closed.

- A proposal for commencing bankruptcy proceedings may be filed by creditors, the debtor himself or a shareholder with personal liability.

- Insolvent debtors or debtors heavily encumbered by debts may suggest compulsory settlement to creditors before the initiation of bankruptcy proceedings.

- Once bankruptcy proceedings have been initiated an insolvent estate is formed, comprising the whole of the debtor's property. In the case of partnerships, this also includes the personal property of personally liable partners.

- All data concerning the initiation and termination of bankruptcy proceedings are entered in the relevant court register.

Bankruptcy proceedings are heard by the competent court in the town where the debtor is located. On the basis of expert opinion, the court may rule that the property of the debtor as a legal person be sold by public auction or call for bids. The decision on the sale of property must specify the following:

- the mode of sale;

- the price;

- terms of payment amount (not less than 10 per cent) and modes for paying deposits, modes of transfer and payment guarantees (not longer than 6 months after the conclusion of the sales agreement).

2.5

Employment Law and Labour Regulations

Jonathan Reuvid

Introduction

Employment law and regulations in the Republic of Slovenia have been harmonized with EC directives as a part of the adoption of the *acquis communautaire* which was the prelude to acceptance as an EU member state from 1 May 2004. This chapter summarizes the key requirements of the law in respect of:

- hiring;

- wages and remuneration;

- termination of employment;

- employment of foreigners.

Hiring

A job opening must be announced publicly. The minimum general requirement is to notify the Employment Agency of the Republic of Slovenia. In certain cases, among others when the prospective employee is a disabled person or when the position is managerial in a private or mixed company, public announcement is not required.

Final candidate selection is made by management or a special committee in accordance with the hiring company's by-laws.

A written employment contract is mandatory. The employee can be hired on a temporary (only under certain conditions) or a permanent basis, with full or part-time employment. A probationary period may be defined in advance.

Wages and remuneration

Minimum wage

The minimum wage for workers, according to their qualifications, is set out by the law or in the Collective Agreement. In the period 2002–4, the minimum gross wage has to be adjusted according to the increase in living costs.

Social security

Workers must pay a total of 22.1 per cent of their gross wages as a contribution for disability assurance and pension, health insurance, unemployment benefit and family leave.

Employers must pay an additional 16.1 per cent on the cost of labour for social security and health insurance cover. They are also obliged to make further payments for the following:

● meals during working hours;

● transportation costs to and from work;

● vacation bonus;

● subsistence and other travel costs;

● difficult working conditions bonuses;

● awards and bonuses for years of service;

● retirement bonuses.

Additional remuneration

Workers are entitled to remuneration in the following circumstances:

● for attending classes or courses which benefit the company;

● during annual leave;

● in the event of illness;

● during maternity/paternity leave; and

● for specific personal reasons (marriage, death within the family, etc).

Termination of employment

Dismissal

Workers may be dismissed for serious infringements of discipline or violating employment obligations, incapacity or insufficient knowledge to perform a job or in cases of redundancy where work cannot be secured for the employee due to technological, organizational or economic reasons. Workers may further be dismissed for committing criminal acts, for not returning to work in accordance with the law, in cases where they are prohibited by the competent authorities to continue working or sent to prison for a period over six months, if the employer is not satisfied with their work during the probationary period, and for not abiding by the instructions of a physician.

Treatment of redundant workers

The procedure for dismissing redundant workers when work cannot be secured for technological, organizational or economic reasons, or as the result of governmental measures, is as follows:

- The employer must inform the trade unions and other workers' representatives of his reasons for reducing the workforce, and of the expected number and categories of redundant workers.

- He must cooperate with trade unions to determine which workers are to be laid off (the law specifies that in this process the efficiency and socio-economic position of workers must be taken into account).

- The employer is obligated to do his utmost for a redundant worker in order to secure for him/her another similar job or to organize retraining.

Employee compensation

During the notice period the employee either works and receives a normal wage or is given compensation in agreement with the employer.

The employee is further entitled to severance pay amounting to a proportion (depending on how long the employee has worked for the employer) of a month's wages for every year worked for the company. At this point, the worker is also entitled to receive monthly unemployment benefits from the Employment Agency. The duration of the benefit depends on the total years of service and the age of the employee, and ranges from three months to two years.

Employment of foreigners

Foreigners can be employed in Slovenia on the basis of a work permit (except in cases stipulated in international agreements). Work permits, valid for one year, are issued by the Employment Agency upon the request of the employer. A foreigner can also apply on his or her own behalf for a so-called personal work permit, which allows the foreigner to be employed by any employer or to be self-employed.

In order for foreigners to stay in the Republic of Slovenia for a period of time greater than that defined in their visa or for reasons different than those defined in their visa (ie foreigners who wish to work in the Republic of Slovenia), a residence permit (that also goes for those foreign nationals who do not require a visa to enter the Republic of Slovenia) must be acquired from the Ministry of Internal Affairs (the application must be filed with the embassy of the Republic of Slovenia in the home country of the foreigner).

Foreigners' wages are governed by the same regulations applicable to domestic employees, and are specified in the employment contract.

Foreign persons with a temporary residence in Slovenia may import goods necessary for their stay; they may import one used (over 6 months old) personal vehicle without paying import duties.

2.6

Competition and Public Procurement

Jonathan Reuvid

Introduction

Slovenia's Law on the Protection of Competition provides protection against unfair competition, dumping and subsidized imports. Prohibited forms of restriction of competition and protection of competition are regulated by the Prevention of Restriction of Competition Act.

The main definition of dumping and subsidizing conforms to that used in the GATT (now WTO) Agreement on Antidumping and the GATT Agreement on Subsidies and Countervailing Measures.

The Republic of Slovenia adopted its first Public Procurement Act in 1997, based on the UNCITRAL model law on the procurement of goods, construction and services. Although the Act was an important new step towards the transparency of process, it gave preference to local bidders against foreign bidders in some circumstances and, therefore, did not harmonize with European Commission directives.

The Law Regulating the Revision of Procedure to Award Public Contracts was adopted, and established the National Auditing Commission for the Auditing of Procedures of Offering Public Tenders, which was introduced in 1999. Finally, in May 2000, Slovenian law on public procurement was brought into line with EU directives with the enactment of a new Public Procurement Act.

Structure

Competition

The Law on the Protection of Competition applies to local and foreign corporate bodies and natural persons engaged in any activity carried out in the market regardless of their legal form of organization and ownership, as well as public companies.

Dumping and subsidized imports

Imported goods are considered to be subsidized if they are given direct or indirect support in production or in export in the country of export or origin.

Goods are deemed to be dumped if their import prices are lower than the 'ordinary price'. Ordinary price refers to a comparable price set for similar goods in the ordinary course of market transactions in the home market of the exporter or any other value established on the basis of international treaties applying to the Republic of Slovenia.

Unfair competition

Prohibited acts of unfair competition encompass any company's acts in the market that are contrary to good practice and will or might cause damage to other participants in the market. In a recent decision the Supreme Court of Slovenia decided that acts of unfair competition can be committed only by the company performing its economic activity. Therefore if an act which is contrary to good practice is made by the company in a market in which it is not a professional player, but, for example, a purchaser or seller of its assets (real estate, shares), such an act cannot be considered an act of unfair competition.

Protection of competition

The Prevention of Restriction of Competition Act applies to all legal and natural persons performing activities in the market for payment, irrespective of their legal status and ownership affiliation, including public undertakings.

Restrictive agreements

Agreements between undertakings, decisions by associations of undertakings and concerted practices regarding business conditions in the market which have as their object or effect the prevention, restriction or distortion of competition are restricted.

Abuse of a dominant position

A dominant position is defined broadly as a situation where a company in the relevant market has no competition or no significant competitors, or when the company has a substantially better position in terms of market shares, financial possibilities, possibilities for purchase or sale or with regard to facts that impede other companies when they enter the market.

Concentrations

Concentrations (mergers, acquisitions, joint ventures and so forth) which strengthen the power of one or more undertakings, individually or jointly, as a result of which effective competition in the relevant market is significantly impeded or excluded, are be prohibited by the law.

Authoritative market restrictions

Regulations, acts and actions are prohibited that:

- prevent the performance of business activities;

- delay the procedure for the issue of relevant permits;

- create discrimination among undertakings with respect to the location of incorporation;

- prohibit trade outside the area of a local community; or

- provide without a justification a specific undertaking with a privileged position.

Public procurement

The provisions of the Public Procurement Act bind contractors, the Republic of Slovenia and its bodies to communicate certain data to the competent bodies of the EU. The provisions relating to the obligation to publish in the *Official Journal of the European Communities* shall begin to apply on 1 May 2004 when the Republic of Slovenia joins the EU.

Practice

Dumping and subsidized imports

In the event of dumped or subsidized imports, the government may, if companies so request, introduce antidumping and countervailing duties if such imports cause or threaten to cause substantial damage to domestic production or hinder the development of domestic production of the same type of goods.

Procedures concerning dumping and subsidized imports fall within the competence of the Competition Protection Office.

Unfair competition

Unfair competition falls within the competence of market inspection. If damages were incurred as a result of an act of unfair competition, they can be claimed in court according to the Obligation code. The affected market participant can also request restitution in a regular litigation procedure.

Restrictive agreements

The Competition Protection Office may issue upon application a negative clearance.

The categories of agreements that do not violate the prohibition are defined by the Decree on Block Exemption. Agreements meeting the conditions determined in the decree do not have to be notified to the Competition Protection Office.

Concentrations

Concentrations have to be notified not more than one week after the signing of a related agreement or announcement of a takeover bid or acquisition of a controlling interest (whichever is sooner) if the aggregate turnover of the undertakings concerned in the Slovenian markets exceeds SIT 8 billion before tax, or the joint market share in the relevant market which will be achieved exceeds 40 per cent.

Public procurement

The Public Procurement Act prescribes the following procedures, which are practically equal to the award-winning procedures regulated by EC directives:

- open procedure;

- restricted procedure for supplier selection;

- negotiated procedure;

- design contest.

A contractor has to publish a tender in the *Official Gazette of the Republic of Slovenia* if the value of the tender exceeds SIT 10 million for goods and services and SIT 20 million for construction works. For low-value contracts below these thresholds contractors must regulate the awarding procedure according to the provisions of the Act.

The Public Procurement Office is responsible for developing the public procurement system so that it ensures rationality, efficiency and transparency in the use of public finances for procurement and encourages competition and the equality of tenderers in public procurement procedures.

Essentials

Unfair competition

Prohibited acts of unfair competition include:

- misleading advertising;
- false information on other companies and products;
- concealing product defects;
- fictitious clearance sales;
- rebates.

Antidumping measures

Antidumping and countervailing duties may not exceed the dumping margin or the value of subsidies and are introduced for the term necessary to neutralize the effects of such imports.

Restrictive agreements

The prohibition on restrictive agreements applies, in particular, to:

- price fixing;
- market sharing;
- market discrimination;
- limitations or control of production, markets, technical development and investment;
- tie-ins.

Abuse of a dominant position

The abuse of a dominant position by one or more companies is prohibited. (Dominance is presumed to exist where a single company's market share exceeds 40 per cent and 60 per cent in the case of joint dominance.)

Concentrations

Mergers, acquisitions and joint ventures, as a result of which effective competition in the relevant market would be significantly impeded or excluded, are prohibited.

Authoritative market restrictions

The government, state and local community institutions, organizations and individuals exercising public authorization are prohibited from restricting the free operation of undertakings in the market with regulations, individual acts or actions.

Public procurement

The Public Procurement Act, which regulates the procurement of goods, services and construction works, also regulates the procedure to be used in public procurement in the water, energy, telecommunications and transport fields in accordance with Slovenia's WTO contracts.

Concerns

Restrictive agreements

Prohibition does not apply to agreements of minor importance, defined as those between undertakings whose aggregate market share does not exceed 5 per cent for horizontal and 10 per cent for vertical agreements.

Abuse of a dominant position

The Competition Protection Officer may issue a negative clearance confirming that a company has not abused its dominant position.

Concentrations

In complicated procedures, the Competition Protection Office may need more time than foreseen by the law (maximum 120 days) to issue clearance. The Competition Protection Office seeks to approve local concentrations, which might lead to limited competition in the market and make entry of foreign competitors difficult, if not impossible. Recently, the Competition Protection Office allowed two mergers leading to near monopolies in the relevant markets.

Authoritative market restrictions

Restriction may be imposed in cases of significant disturbances in the market or in supply as a result of a natural disaster, epidemic, state of emergency.

Part Three

Finance, Accountancy and Taxation

3.1

Financial Services

Viktor Lence, Postna banka Slovenije d.d. (Post Bank of Slovenia)

Introduction

During the past decade, the Slovene financial sector, as well as the whole economy in Slovenia, has passed through many changes. The performance of the economy during this period was characterized mainly by the transition process of setting up a market economy, privatization of economic entities and promotion of private initiative. Slovenia has entered the final process of integration with the EU in 2004 and is preparing itself to enter the monetary union in 2008. Slovenia has proven to be the most developed among the group of potential new member countries. Accordingly, it was awarded the highest credit rating in the region, which was improved further in June 2003.

During the forthcoming period, the country is facing the following main challenges:

- restructuring of the manufacturing sector and improvement of competitiveness;

- establishment of a transparent capital market;

- privatization of the financial sector (banking and insurance sectors in particular);

- improved quality of management, which is especially an issue in the newly privatized enterprises;

- promotion of entrepreneurship.

Financial institutions – a general description

Financial institutions are important elements of any modern market economy. Their successful performance is a condition for the current operation of the economy as a whole. Key to the importance of their fundamental function of transforming the quality of assets is their ability to process information adequately, which enables them to define and manage risks effectively.

In the process of integration into the European Union and, consequently, opening the market to free competition, the need for them to be effective has increased. That need is strengthened by privatization, market concentration – economies of scale – and the entrance of foreign owners from developed markets.

During the period of establishment of a market economy, the number of financial institutions in Slovenia grew as a result of newly established entities entering the market and through the establishment of new financial market segments (investment funds, mutual funds, brokerage companies and investment companies). However, since 1997 the number of financial institutions has decreased. Mutual funds represent the only exception to this trend, having increased both in number and, particularly, in the volume of the assets they manage. The market for supplementary pension insurance was established as late as 2000, when the first pension companies were formed and mutual pension funds designed. The decline in the number of Slovene financial institutions in the five years from 1997 to 2002 is analysed in Table 3.1.1.

Table 3.1.1 Number of financial institutions in Slovenia

Types of financial institutions	31 Dec. 1997	31 Dec. 2002
Monetary financial institutions		
Banks	28	20
Savings banks	62	
Savings and loan undertakings	70	28
Non-monetary financial institutions		
Brokerage companies*	43	17
Management companies	26	19
Investment companies (funds)	60	33
Mutual funds	15	18
Insurance companies	13	11
Re-insurance companies	2	2
Pension companies	–	6
Mutual pension funds	–	6

*Together with 11 banks licensed for performing securities operations.
Source: Bank of Slovenia

Banks

The Slovene banking sector is relatively well developed, but there are still numerous opportunities for its further development. At the beginning of the 1990s, after the transition to market economy status, the state turned the largest banks round, cleared their bad investments and took over ownership. At the same time, there were several new banks established by either domestic entities or foreign investors coming mainly from the neighbouring countries. The privatization process of the state-owned banks has been implemented gradually; as Table 3.1.2 reveals, the process has not yet been accomplished.

Table 3.1.2 Ownership structure of the Slovene banking sector *

	31 Dec. 2000	30 Jun. 2002
Foreign entities	12%	21.1%
States in a narrow sense	37%	35.8%
Other domestic entities	51%	43.1%

* Measured by ownership capital
Source: Bank of Slovenia

In Slovenia, the banks are predominantly privately owned. Exceptions to this rule are the two largest banks taken over by the state during their rehabilitation, and two smaller banks. The savings banks are entirely owned by private domestic owners. After the last changes in bank ownership structure, the proportion of banks in foreign ownership in Slovenia is approaching a figure typical for developed Western European countries.

The number of banks, savings banks and savings and loan undertakings has been decreasing for several years. In 1994, there were 34 banks operating in Slovenia; in 1997 there were still 28, and in 2002 only 20 banks were left. In particular, the process of larger banks absorbing smaller ones was prevalent. A very high number of savings and loan undertakings used to operate in Slovenia, but all of them together did not account for a high market share. Their number has decreased rapidly owing to the demand for alignment of their operations with bank regulations, and they have merged with banks or savings banks.

The decreasing number of banks has led to increased concentration in the banking sector. In 2001, the market share of the largest bank, measured by the aggregate balance of its accounts, increased from 29 per cent to 35 per cent, of the three largest banks from 50 per cent to 56 per cent, and of the first seven banks from 73 per cent to 80 per cent.

The financial sector has developed in step with the development of the whole economy. It has gained in importance through the deepening financial market. At the end of 1995, the total balance of accounts in all banks reached 67 per cent of gross domestic product (GDP), and on 31 December 2001 it amounted to 87 per cent of GDP. Compared with the banks from the developed countries of Western Europe, there is plenty of room left for further development of the financial sector in Slovenia, either through growth in the volume of financial transactions, or through enlarging the range of services. Such development, however, takes time and has to be based on the real needs and requirements of the business sector. In Slovenia, development in this particular field seems to be significant.

In recent years, the proportion of long-term assets in the structure of the banks' balance sheets has grown, resulting from increased domestic savings and resources acquired from abroad. A better country credit rating enables the Slovene banks to acquire cheaper resources abroad, particularly in the form of syndicated loans, while the banks in foreign ownership obtain assets from their foreign mother-banks. This is considered a basis for the growth of the banks' potential for loans on a long-term basis. Such funds are particularly important for the promotion of promising company development projects in non-banking sectors.

The population's debt with the banks is low. The ratio of loans to deposits has reached 0.29. The banks can consider this fact as a suitable lever for their potential growth – particularly because mortgage lending in Slovenia is not yet developed. A regulation is being prepared to set up mortgage banking. This framework is expected to facilitate a more significant development of loans for real estate and dwellings.

In Slovenia, the national motorway construction programme has been in progress for several years, and is heavily financed by domestic banks. This national project is a strong lever to keep a higher economic growth rate. The stimulation of European transport flows will have a long-term positive impact on the country's economic activities.

In Slovenia, the banks have developed an array of services which are, to a great extent, comparable to the offerings of banks from the European Union. In the field of retail operations, the various modern types of payment instruments and market trends are very well developed and used extensively.

There are many payment cards issued within the country's total population of two million and their usage is growing fast. Among the 650,000 credit cards in issue, 60 per cent are domestic and 40 per cent licensed and issued on the basis of an acquired foreign licence. The banks have issued 70 per cent of all credit cards; the balance of 30 per cent is company cards issued by non-banks. The number of debit cards now exceeds 900,000. Within the country, payment of goods and services by cards can be made at over 13,000 outlets equipped with point-of-sale (POS) terminals. Some of them also provide cash advances. There are almost 700 automatic teller machines (ATMs) placed in the country, which provide coverage of fewer than 3,000 persons per ATM. Numerous financial services are accessible at 550 post offices throughout the whole country.

Insurance

In Slovenia, the insurance market is generally less developed than in the European Union, but it is growing fast, in terms of both insurance products offered and volume of insurance premiums paid. The development of the insurance industry is shown both by the growth of total premiums paid and by increased insurance expenditure per capita. A higher rate of growth is expected in the life insurance market.

In 2002, there were 11 insurance companies and two re-insurance companies operating in Slovenia. The majority of the insurance companies deal with property and life insurance; one of them specializes in health insurance only. The Slovene insurance market is highly concentrated. In 2002, the largest insurance company's market share, measured by the criterion of aggregate gross premiums, reached 43 per cent, and the combined market shares of the three largest insurance companies amounted to 78 per cent.

Slovenska izvozna družba (Slovene Export Corporation), which deals with insurance of export businesses against commercial and non-commercial risks, is especially noteworthy; it provides important support for companies extending their operations through export to new markets abroad.

The process of privatizing insurance companies is in progress. As a first stage, the unregistered share capital of insurance companies is ascertained, and then shares are transferred to beneficiaries entitled to privatization of the unregistered capital. The proportion of foreign capital in the ownership structure of Slovene insurance companies has reached 27 per cent, which is comparable to the majority of countries within the EU.

Additional voluntary pension insurance

The pension reform which started in 2000 introduced voluntary pension insurance in addition to compulsory insurance within the state institutions. At the end of 2002, additional voluntary pension insurance was offered by six mutual pension funds, six pension companies and three insurance companies. The process of concentration in this new growing market has already begun.

Investment funds

Investment funds formation dates back to the period of massive privatization of economic entities at the beginning of the 1990s. The former
state ownership in companies operating in the non-financial sectors was
in most cases transferred by vouchers to the investment companies;
Slovene citizens, the voucher owners, became the investors. In 2003,
the investment companies have to be transformed either into ordinary
investment companies (as they are known in market economies) or into
regular joint-stock companies or financial holding companies.

The first mutual funds were established a little later. In line with
the development of the capital market, their number is increasing, while
the number of investors and the volume of resources invested in these
funds are also growing considerably.

At the end of 2002, 19 management companies managed 18 mutual
funds and 33 investment companies, of which the number is decreasing
due to concentration and their transformation into joint-stock companies.

Leasing

In Slovenia, there are 32 providers of leasing services. This is a market
of high volume growth. At present, the leasing of movables and, within
that, the leasing of motor cars predominates, but the share of real estate
leasing is also increasing.

Securities market

The securities market in Slovenia was re-established after almost 50
years along with the process of privatizing state property and the setting
up of a regular market economy. Ljubljanska borza vrednostnih papirjev
(the Ljubljana Stock Exchange) was established in December 1989 as a
form of transparent and organized securities market.

In 1995, Centralna klirinško depotna družba (Central Clearing
Deposit Company) started its operations; it maintains the register of
issued non-materialized securities and organizes the safe clearing of
pecuniary liabilities arising from transactions in securities concluded
in the organized market.

At the end of 2002, 28 authorized participants operated in the Slovene
financial market, of which 11 were banks and 17 brokerage companies.
The latter were engaged in brokerage operations, while the banks
operated in addition with their own investments.

At the same date, 1,032 securities of 870 issuers were registered in
the Central Clearing Deposit Company, on the Stock Exchange – as
the organized market, where 197 issuers dealt in 264 securities, compris-

ing 172 quoted shares and 92 listed bonds. Total market capitalization amounted to 43 per cent of GDP. During 2002, the value of the Slovene Stock Exchange Index (SBI) increased by 55 per cent.

About 40 per cent of the trade in shares and bonds is still performed in securities not quoted on the stock exchange, in the so-called 'grey' market. This fact reduces the transparency of the market and securities pricing. In Slovenia, the primary securities market has developed weakly. In addition to state bonds, some closed issues, mostly of bonds, appear occasionally.

Statutory regulation

During the period of transformation of the Slovene economy to a market economy, the process needed to be supported by appropriate legislation. In the legislative sphere, it was necessary to modify many regulations and laws or to adopt completely new ones. Only company management is newly regulated, while in the financial domain legislation to regulate banking, insurance operations, the securities market, investment funds and some other segments of the financial sector was drawn up. During the gradual progression to a market economy, the legislation was also transformed. The process was based primarily on the European Union *acquis communautaire*.

During the period of preparation for integration into the EU, a comprehensive alignment of regulations to the EU legislation and directives is also in progress. This alignment has been developed in compliance with the obligations adopted under the signed Association Agreement.

Accountancy

Like the alignment of legislation, the new market economy also demands that companies align the management of their accounting. In 2002, the renewed Slovene Accounting Standards came into force, mostly summarizing the solutions from International Accounting Standards (IAS). Accounting solutions, standards, external audit practices and disclosures requested in reports function on behalf of shareholders and the business partners of companies.

Supervision

The financial services market is associated with specific risks, and this is the reason for legislation specifically drawn up to regulate the entry of new participants (licensing) and for supervision of the performance of active participants in financial markets. There are three independent legal entities operating in Slovenia, supervising individual segments of the financial system: the banking sector, the insurance sector and the securities market.

The Bank of Slovenia, as central bank, supervises all other banks and savings banks and monitors the alignment of savings and loan undertakings to bank regulations. It is independent in its work.

The Securities Market Agency supervises brokerage companies, investment funds and mutual pension fund operations, as well as their management. In addition, it supervises operations of the Ljubljana Stock Exchange and Central Clearing Deposit Company.

The Insurance Supervision Agency supervises the operation of insurance companies and re-insurance companies, the performance of the insurance activities of the Slovene Export Corporation, and the operations of pension companies and some other special institutions.

Both agencies mentioned above are also independent in their work. In order to provide more effective supervision over the financial institutions, these three supervisory bodies, although independent, cooperate mutually in conformity with the rules on mutual cooperation among supervisory bodies, and by mutual agreement. Such agreements have likewise been concluded with foreign supervisory institutions. They also cooperate with external auditors.

Summary

The financial services sector in Slovenia has been entirely transformed over the past 10 years, and in some segments designed completely anew. In line with the market economy's expansion, the financial sector has also experienced boom development. Growth is present in all segments and particularly visible in some of them, which provides significant opportunities for market players. The processes of privatization and concentration have been developed simultaneously. The boom in the financial services sector has been accompanied by statutory regulation alignment and the development of supervisory institutions.

Accounting and Audit

Deloitte & Touche Central Europe

Introduction

Slovenian Accounting Standards were derived from International Accounting Standards and the directives of the European Union, especially the 4th and 7th Directives. On 1 January 2002, new Slovenian Accounting Standards were introduced.

Structure

Accounting companies are obliged to keep their books of business and develop final accounts of business transactions in accordance with the accounting principles and standards adopted by an expert organization, ie the Association of Accountants and Auditors of Slovenia.

The Accounting Act also regulates bookkeeping and the elaboration of annual reports of budget users, legal entities of public law and legal entities of private law that do not keep books according to the Act on Commercial Companies.

Auditing

The Auditing Act provides for the harmonization of the Slovenian accounting and auditing profession with the requirements of Directive VIII of the EU and IFAC (International Federation of Accountants).

Practice

Each company is required to prepare a final account which contains a balance sheet, a profit and loss account, annexures and an annual report on the status of the company: optional but recommended is a net cash-flow statement. The Act prescribes minimal data for balance sheets, profit and loss accounts, annexures and annual reports on business transactions. Companies are divided into small, medium and large ones according to criteria of the 4th Directive of the European Union. Consolidated final accounts are to be made by associated companies as stated in the 7th Directive of the European Union.

Auditing

Companies for which auditing is compulsory will be required to submit financial statements to the authorized auditors registered and supervised by the Slovenian Institute for Auditing.

Compulsory auditing under the Companies Act applies to large and medium joint-stock companies, large limited liability companies, associated (affiliated) companies, and companies whose shares or bonds are floated on the Ljubljana Stock Exchange.

Essentials

The entire accounting activity regulated by Slovenian accounting standards focuses on the preparation of financial statements for a number of users. The management of an enterprise may have prepared financial statements for its own use in more than one way, depending on specific internal management requirements. If financial statements are also published for other persons (shareholders, creditors, employees, the general public), they should be prepared in compliance with the international accounting standards upon which the Slovenian accounting standards are based.

Accounting information in a group of related enterprises

A group of related enterprises for which a consolidated balance sheet and a consolidated profit and loss statement should be prepared comprises a parent company together with the subsidiaries in which the company has:

- an absolute majority of shareholders' votes or members of annual shareholders' meetings;

- the right to appoint an absolute majority of members of the board of directors, the management board, or the supervisory board, and holds shares, capital interests and similar;

- at least 20 per cent of the shares and the majority of members of the board of directors, the management board, or the supervisory board appointed exclusively to execute its voting rights;

- the power to govern and control the above governing bodies but does not hold shares, capital interests and the like; or

- an absolute majority of voting rights and/or members of annual shareholders' meetings by virtue of an agreement with other investors; or

- at least 20 per cent of the shares and has *de facto* power to govern or control or is, together with the first company, governed by the second company.

A parent company that is itself a subsidiary does not have to prepare consolidated financial statements provided the relevant approval has been obtained from minority interest holders.

The financial statements of a subsidiary should be excluded from consolidation when: 1) control by the parent company is intended to be temporary because the subsidiary has been acquired and is being held exclusively with a view to its subsequent disposal in the near future; or 2) it operates under severe long-term restrictions which significantly impair its ability to transfer funds to the parent.

Consolidated financial statements should be prepared and presented as those of a single enterprise.

Auditing

According to the Auditing Act, auditing companies have to be established in compliance with the Commercial Companies Act, which means that auditing companies can be established as one of the following forms:

- Partnerships (organized according to general provisions of continental law):

  - limited partnership;

  - general partnership;

  - silent partnership.

- Corporate forms:

  - joint stock company;

  - limited liability company;

  - limited partnership by shares (German model).

The activity of auditing may also be performed by a sole proprietor.

Share owners who participate in equity and management on the basis of those shares with minimum of 75 per cent have to be authorized auditors, auditing companies, auditing companies of member states of the EU or foreign auditing companies. The principle of reciprocity applies for foreign auditing companies.

An auditing company should employ at least one authorized auditor (certified public accountant) registered with the Slovenian Institute for Auditing and having obtained certification from the Institute.

3.3

Taxation

Deloitte & Touche Central Europe

Summary of taxation in Slovenia

The tax system consists of three main categories of taxes:

- direct taxes on income;
- direct taxes on property;
- indirect taxes.

All taxes are collected by the Tax Administration of the Republic of Slovenia, except for customs duties, excise duties and value added tax on imports, which are collected by the Customs Administration of the Republic of Slovenia.

Corporate income tax

Corporate income tax (CIT) is levied on the taxable profit of private companies at a rate of 25 per cent, with a 10 per cent tax rate applying to corporations established in the Special Economic Zones. Depreciation allowances are quite favourable on buildings (5 per cent) and machinery and equipment (33 per cent). A general investment incentive applies regardless of the scale of operation, ie a deduction from the tax base of 40 per cent of the investment in the year of investment, and an allowance for 10 per cent of profits placed tax free into an investment reserve.

Dividends

The paying company withholds tax (CIT or PIT) at a 25 per cent rate on each distributed dividend to a resident of Slovenia and 15 per cent on dividends transferred abroad, unless otherwise provided for by a tax treaty. If corporate tax was previously imposed, there is no with-holding tax on dividends distributed to a Slovenian resident who is a legal entity.

Personal income tax

Personal income tax (PIT) applies to an individual's income. There are six categories of income: income from employment, pensions and other receipts, income from private business or professional activity, income from agriculture, income from property, income from property rights and capital gains. The taxable income of an individual, earned in a calendar year, is aggregated and the total amount is taxed at progressive rates. Personal allowances are taken into account when making the assessment of the amount of tax to be paid, and compulsory social security contributions are deducted along with certain expenses. There are six tax brackets with rates of: 17 per cent, 35 per cent, 37 per cent, 40 per cent, 45 per cent and 50 per cent. Advance tax payments during the tax period are deductible from the final tax liability and any difference is collected on receipt of an assessment from the tax authorities. When the total sum of advance payments exceeds the tax payable, a refund can be requested. Advance tax payments on salaries, wages, pensions, income from agriculture and income from private business or professional activity (with the exception of certain professional or business activities) are determined according to the special tax rate scales. The rate of advance tax payment on income earned under contracts for temporary work or for the performance of services, and other receipts including prizes and similar receipts, income from property and income from property rights is 25 per cent. The rate of advance tax payment on capital gains is 30 per cent.

Non-residents are liable to income tax on certain Slovenian source income. If they resided in Slovenia for less than six consecutive months, they don't have to fill the final tax return. In that case the tax paid in Slovenia is treated as a final tax.

Non-residents can be taxed for the withholding tax for the income gained in Slovenia.

Payroll tax

The payroll tax is levied on the gross salary or wage payments of employees who are obliged to pay social security contributions under special law. It is levied at progressive rates of 0 per cent, 3.8 per cent, 7.8 per cent and 14.8 per cent. Companies employing disabled individuals representing at least 40 per cent of the total workforce during the entire business year are exempted from paying this tax.

Contractual work tax

This tax is levied on gross payments made to individuals performing temporary contractual work at a rate of 25 per cent. Payments for certain types of contractual work are exempted.

Social security contributions

Besides personal income tax, individuals must pay compulsory social security contributions. Contributions must be paid by both employer and employee, with the contributions withheld by the employer. Self-employed persons must pay income tax and social security contributions by themselves. There are four types of contributions paid to two social security schemes and to the state budget as follows:

- for pension and disability insurance, paid to the Pension Fund;

- for medical care and sickness leave, paid to the Health Fund;

- for unemployment insurance, paid to the state budget; and

- for maternity leave, paid to the state budget.

Value added tax

Value added tax (VAT) is a general consumption tax on a net basis included in the price consumers pay for goods and services. Consumers pay this tax indirectly, and a taxable company or person engaging in commercial activity must remit the tax to the Tax Administration Office. All companies pay VAT except those carrying out certain defined activities, small businesses and farmers with a turnover and income below defined thresholds and those dealing with products intended for export and international transport. There are two VAT rates: a general rate of 20 per cent, and a reduced rate of 8.5 per cent.

Excise duties

Excise duties are levied on alcohol and alcoholic beverages, mineral oils, gas and manufactured tobacco. Those liable to pay excise duties are the manufacturers, the importers of products and the persons to whom the liability may be transferred. Products intended for export are exempted.

Tax on insurance premiums

This tax is levied on insurance premiums and paid by insurance companies. The tax rate is 6.5 per cent.

Immovable property transfer tax

Tax is levied on the seller on the amount of the transaction at a rate of 2 per cent. There are exemptions for certain types of immovable property.

Customs duties

Customs duties are levied on imported goods. This amounts to a percentage of the value of the goods being imported. Tariff rates for industrial goods range from 0 to 27 per cent. For some agricultural products tariff rates are higher. Slovenia has concluded several free trade agreements (with the EU, CEFTA, EFTA, Croatia and others) and goods imported from these countries are taxed at preferential rates. Goods imported temporarily can be totally or partially exempt from customs duties according to relevant customs procedures.

Corporate income tax

All legal persons carrying out commercial activities and having their head office in Slovenia (partnerships and other corporate forms, investment funds, banks, insurance companies, cooperative enterprises, public enterprises and other legal persons) are subject to corporate income tax. Non-residents (legal persons who do not have their headquarters in Slovenia) are subject to corporate income tax to the extent that the income is the result of carrying out business activity in Slovenia. If a permanent operating unit of a foreign entity is regulated otherwise in an agreement on avoidance of double taxation, the provisions of that agreement apply.

There are a limited number of legal persons who are exempted from corporation tax, for example the Bank of Slovenia, investment funds (if they distribute 90 per cent of the past year's profit by 30 November of the current year), and non-profit and charitable organizations.

The general corporate profits tax rate is 25 per cent, although a reduced tax rate of 10 per cent applies under certain conditions to companies performing business activities in the Special Economic Zones and to the extent the income is generated from these activities.

The tax is levied on net profits, defined according to the profit and loss account, as revenue minus expenditure. Taxable income includes receipts which are determined according to the regulations or accounting standards. This generally includes all income received and capital gains realized. The expenditures of the taxpayer include the expenses allowed by regulations or accounting standards, except those which are determined in a different manner under the Profits Tax Act. Allowable expenditures include only those expenses which represent a direct expense for the performance of an activity for the production of income. They do not include expenses in the form of investments. Other non-deductible expenses include: provision against potential losses; interest on arrears for delayed payment of taxes and contributions; claims written off against workers, owners or associated persons; and fines.

Expenditure on plant and machinery generally qualifies for annual writing-down allowances. The depreciation allowances on buildings and equipment are quite favourable. Depreciation may not exceed the level arrived at using straight-line depreciation methods and the set annual depreciation rates shown in Table 3.3.1.

Table 3.3.1 Depreciation allowances

Depreciation group	Highest annual depreciation rates (%)
1. Building structures	5
2. Equipment	25
3. Personal vehicles	12.5
4. Computers and computer equipment	50
5. Perennial plants	10
6. Foundation stocks	20
7. Other investments	20
8. Goodwill	10

The taxpayer can choose the method of valuing inventories (stock) between FIFO, LIFO, weighted average price or moving average price. When the method of valuation is changed, the taxpayer must explain in the tax report the reasons for such a change and its fiscal effects.

Losses may be offset against taxable profits in the following five years (except in the case of mergers and group taxation). A carry-back of losses is not permitted. Losses are computed in the same way as profits, and any losses realized must be declared in the tax return.

Capital gains from selling equity or capital assets are subject to tax without exemption.

There are a number of adjustments or limitations imposed on deductible expenses:

• Interest, other than interest on loans obtained from owners or associated persons, is limited to the level of the average inter-bank annual interest rate.

• Salaries are determined by the collective labour agreements.

• Severance compensation for pensioners, holiday cash grants, solidarity aid, subsidized meals, salaries of trainees, awards in connection with anniversaries, business travel and other allowances in connection with work are allowable to the extent set by the government.

• Long-term reserves for future material and non-material costs and allocations to the investment reserve are partially deductible.

• Entertainment expenses, and expenses for management and auditing boards are limited to 70 per cent of their total amount.

• Donations for humanitarian, cultural, scientific, educational, sports, ecological and religious purposes are limited to a maximum 0.3 per cent of realized income.

Two important tax incentives apply: a general investment incentive regardless of the scale of operation, ie a deduction from the tax base of the investment in the year of investment, and an allowance of 10 per cent of profits placed tax free into an investment reserve. The latter allowance can be granted for a four-year term.

There are two further general tax incentives for entities that provide work for a trainee or a previously unemployed person and for those employing disabled people. The total cumulative allowances should not exceed the amount of the tax base.

Below you can find detailed descriptions of mentioned incentives.

Reserves for future investments can be created by the taxpayer. Up to 10 per cent of taxable income can be allocated to the reserve and be deducted from the tax base. After a two-year period, unused funds in the reserve must be taken into accounts as taxable income.

The Slovenian Corporate income tax law provides an *investment allowance* of up to 30 per cent of the amount invested in fixed assets (except for personal cars) and long-term intangible assets that is deductible from the investor's taxable income, provided that the amount does not exceed the tax base, and an additional 10 per cent of the amount invested in equipment (except for personal cars, furniture and other office equipment) and long-term intangible assets. This incentive does not influence the depreciation value (actually up to 140 per cent of the investment is tax deductible in the years of depreciation).

A taxpayer using this investment allowance may not allocate profit for profit sharing (for three years); if a taxpayer does allocate profit from this year for profit sharing within three years after the year in which the tax allowance was used, the taxpayer must increase the tax base (for the allowance) in the current year. The assets for which the allowance was used should not be disposed of until three years after the allowance was used. If the assets are disposed of within three years the tax base should be increased for the allowance.

The above-mentioned percentages apply in 2003. In future the incentive percentages will be lower.

Employment incentive – a company can deduct 30 per cent of the gross salary earned by a person who is just entering the workforce, a previously unemployed person, or a trainee for a position, during the first twelve months of employment, from its taxable income. The employment must be for an unlimited period or for a fixed period of at least two years.

Business organizations established in the Special Economic Zones are entitled to additional tax incentives, including a lower corporate income tax rate (10 per cent), an additional 50 per cent tax relief on investment into fixed assets and a reduction of the tax basis to 50 per cent of the salaries paid out to new employees (see final paragraph of this chapter).

Corporate income tax is payable during the fiscal year, which is a calendar year. Tax payments must be made in advance (monthly or four times in the year) and be proportionate to the level of the tax base in the latest assessment. Statements on taxable income must be presented with the tax returns prescribed by the Ministry of Finance. The statements can be based on consolidated accounts if the resident taxpayer owns more than 90 per cent of another resident taxpayer's share capital. In the case of non-resident taxpayers no group tax treatment is allowed. Tax returns must be submitted to the tax authorities by 31 March of the current year for the preceding year, and joint tax returns must be filed by 15 April.

The tax administration has the discretionary power to select taxpayers for audit examination and taxable persons have the right of administrative appeal on all decisions. The assessments and results of an audit issued by the tax administration must take place within 15 days. An appeal to court can also be made.

Dividends

The paying company withholds tax at 25 per cent on each distributed (paid-out) dividend to a resident of Slovenia and at 15 per cent on each distributed dividend to a non-resident unless otherwise provided by a tax treaty. However, to mitigate double taxation of the same stream of profits which would arise if profits were taxed once in the hands of the company and again when distributed to shareholders as dividends if corporate tax was previously imposed on profit from which dividends are paid, there is no withholding tax on dividends paid to corporate income taxpayers who are residents of Slovenia.

Interest and royalties

There is no withholding tax imposed on interests and royalties paid to residents' and non-residents' companies and legal entities.

Double taxation agreements

Double taxation agreements (DTAs) lay down rules for the taxation of income or capital crossing international frontiers. They define taxing rights between two countries to prevent international double taxation.

DTAs contribute to eliminating obstacles to the flow of goods, services, capital, persons and technology. Slovenia is a very open economy and pursues a policy that encourages cross-border economic activity by providing for certainty in tax treatment. Slovenia, when establishing DTAs, uses the uniform basis of the OECD Model Tax Convention on Income and Capital.

After gaining independence in 1991, Slovenia has ratified bilaterally with other countries the DTAs concluded by the Former Republic of Yugoslavia listed in Table 3.3.2.

Table 3.3.2 Slovenia's DTAs carried forward from Republic of Yugoslavia

Treaty country	Tax covered
Belgium	Income and capital
China	Income
Cyprus	Income and capital
Czechoslovakia	Income and capital
Denmark	Income and capital
Egypt	Income and capital
Finland	Income and capital
France	Income
Germany	Income and capital
Greece	Income from air and sea transport
Hungary	Income and capital
Italy	Income and capital
Malaysia	Income
Netherlands	Income and capital
Norway	Income and capital
Philippines	Income
Romania	Income and capital
Sri Lanka	Income and capital
Sweden	Income and capital
United Kingdom	Income

Slovenia started to negotiate in its own right in 1993 and has concluded additional DTAs with the countries listed in Table 3.3.3.

Table 3.3.3 DTAs negotiated by Slovenia since 1993

Treaty country	Tax covered
Austria	Income and capital
China	Income and capital
Czech Republic	Income and capital
Poland	Income and capital
Russian Federation	Income and capital
Switzerland	Income and capital
Macedonia	Income and capital
United States	Income and capital
Luxemburg	Income and capital
Belgium	Income and capital

Withholding taxes

Approach to distributed profits

The paying company withholds tax at 25 per cent on each distributed (paid-out) dividend to a resident of Slovenia and at 15 per cent on each distributed dividend to a non-resident, unless otherwise provided by a tax treaty. However, if corporate tax of 25 per cent was previously imposed. on profit from which dividends are paid, there is no withholding tax on dividends paid to corporate income taxpayers who are residents of Slovenia.

Non-residents entitled to a lower tax rate according to a DTA have the right to request the refund of overpaid tax from the tax authorities.

Approach to interests and royalties

No withholding tax is imposed on interests and royalties paid to resident and non-resident legal entities.

Partnerships

The taxable base of a general or limited partnership is computed initially for the partnership as a whole under the rules applicable to companies. For general partnerships, the resulting profit or loss is divided between the partners in accordance with the partnership level as a legal entity, and the distributions of profit to the limited partners are taxed again as income from participation in profit at the rate of 25 per cent.

Non-resident companies

Legal entities that do not have their head office in the Republic of Slovenia are treated as non-residents and taxed on the profits derived by carrying out activities on a permanent basis in Slovenia.

Other profit taxes

No other profit taxes are currently levied in Slovenia.

Indirect taxation – VAT

The value added tax is regulated by the Law on Value Added Tax (*Official Gazette* No. 89/98, 23 December 1998). The law entered into force on 1 July 1999.

Taxable transactions

The VAT is imposed on supplies of goods and services, unless specifically exempted, including immovable property, and on imports.

The supply of services means any transaction which does not constitute a supply of goods.

Taxable persons

A taxable person is any person who makes taxable supplies independently. Taxable persons are liable to pay tax on all amounts received or receivable by them for taxable supplies made in the course of their business, trade or similar activity.

Taxable persons must register as taxable persons if the value of their supplies within the period of the last 12 months exceeds the threshold of SIT 5,000,000 (approximately EUR 25,000).

The limit for entry to the VAT system for agricultural activities is SIT 1,500,000 (approximately EUR 8,000), in accordance with the cadastral income of agricultural and forestry land.

Place of supply

The place of supply of goods is located where the goods are delivered, made available or handed over or, for goods that are transported, at the place where the transportation starts. If goods are to be assembled or installed, the place of supply is the place where the goods are assembled or installed.

In general, the place of supply of services is located where the person performing a service is established or has his or her permanent office. Special rules apply to services performed in connection with immovable property, transport services, etc. A reverse charge rule is defined for certain services provided by persons not established within the tax territory of Slovenia. These services include services with respect to property rights, advertising services, services of consultants, lawyers, etc.

Time of supply

VAT is charged when goods are delivered or when services are performed. It is considered that this happens when a VAT invoice is issued for the supply. The invoice must be issued within 8 days after delivering goods or services. If an invoice is not issued, VAT shall be charged on the eighth day after the delivery of goods or services.

When payments are made in advance, the VAT applies to those payments as they are made.

Continuing services are deemed to be supplied on the last day of the tax period to which the invoice or payment relates.

VAT on importation of goods is chargeable when the goods are brought into the territory of the Republic of Slovenia. When goods are placed under a procedure other than release for free circulation or temporary admission with partial exemption from customs duties, the tax will become chargeable whereby the goods cease to be covered by these arrangements.

When imported goods are subject to import duties, the VAT is chargeable when those duties become chargeable.

Taxable amount

The tax is imposed on the payment that a supplier receives or is entitled to receive as a result of the supply. The value includes all forms of payment, in cash or in kind, whether paid by the customer or by a third person.

The taxable amount includes incidental expenses such as commissions, packaging costs, transport and insurance as well as taxes, duties, and charges other than the VAT.

For imported goods the taxable amount is the value of goods determined in accordance with customs regulation, increased by customs duties and other duties paid upon importation, VAT excluded.

VAT rates

The Law on Value Added Tax sets two VAT rates: the standard VAT rate is 20 per cent and the reduced rate is 8.5 per cent. The reduced rate is imposed particularly on supply of the following:

● foodstuffs, including food services in restaurants;

● agricultural inputs;

● water;

● pharmaceutical products;

● medical equipment, accessories for the handicapped;

● public passenger transport;

● books, newspapers and periodicals;

● services of authors, composers;

● cultural events;

● sporting events and facilities;

● housing, hotel and like accommodation; and

● funerals.

Exemptions

Exemptions are divided into:

● activities in the public interest;

● public postal services;

- hospital and medical care;

- medical services; human organs, blood and milk;

- welfare and social security work;

- school or university education,

- sport or physical education;

- organizations with aims of a political, trade-union, religious, philosophical or civil nature;

- cultural services and public radio and television broadcasts.

Other activities:

- insurance and reinsurance;

- immovable properties, except newly constructed;

- letting of residential houses and apartments;

- financial services;

- postage stamps and similar stamps;

- betting, gambling and lotteries.

There are also:

- exemptions on importation of goods;

- exemptions on export of goods and international transport;

- other special exemptions linked to international goods traffic.

Export of goods is defined as the supply of goods dispatched or transported to a destination outside the Republic of Slovenia by or on behalf of a taxable person.

Assessment

VAT must be paid by the end of the month following the end of each tax period. If VAT is not paid within the time limit prescribed, fines and penalty interest are chargeable.

Taxable persons have to calculate tax liability and submit a tax return for a tax period that is a calendar month, calendar quarter or half a calendar year. Tax credits (excess of input tax over output tax in the tax period) can be carried forward to the following VAT tax period. However, any VAT registered taxable person is entitled to a refund within 60 days after submission of a VAT tax return form, except for exporters, who are entitled to a refund within 30 days after submission of a VAT tax return form.

Small businesses

Small businesses with a turnover below the limit of SIT 5,000,000 (approximately EUR 26,900) are not liable to VAT.

They may opt to register as a VAT taxable person. If they are registered, the registration must be valid for at least a five-year period. There are no special rules regarding tax reporting and accounting for small businesses.

Tax refund

Foreign buyers are entitled to a tax refund (except on mineral oils, tobacco products and alcoholic beverages) when the value of goods exceeds SIT 15,000. A tax refund is possible within 6 months from the date of filing the refund claim.

Forthcoming tax system reforms

The Slovenian tax system is further evolving to close existing loopholes and move towards full harmonization with EU tax systems. The government of Slovenia is committed to joining the EU by the end of May 2005. Accordingly, the tax system will be further adjusted to comply with the remaining EU tax directives.

Given the strategic tax policy objectives pursued, the *corporate income tax* should be adjusted. In particular, special attention should be given to closing existing loopholes in the present system by introducing source taxation for income that is comparable to that in OECD countries, studying the idea of raising the tax rate for distributed profits and lowering the tax rate for undistributed profits. At the same time, the following three directives on corporate income tax will be included in the law:

● the merger directive;

● the parent and subsidiary directive; and

● the indirect taxes on the raising of capital.

The proposal has not been published yet and it is expected that the changes will be effective from 1 January 2005 rather than 1 January 2004. So far, only some of the solutions proposed by the Ministry of Finance are known. Some that should be of interest to foreign investors are:

● The depreciation rates for certain assets should be lowered.

● The investment incentive should be lowered to 20 per cent and the amount should lower the depreciation base.

- The tax rate should remain the same.

- Withholding taxes on certain services, interest, and royalties charged from abroad (from legal entities not resident in Slovenia) should be introduced (at the time the rate of 25 per cent is proposed, but should, according to our expectations, be significantly lowered).

- Personal income tax should be revised. Special attention will be given to widening the taxable base (precision of source rules). Additionally, the shift from general allowances to tax credits is expected in connection with the reduction of the tax burden on low-income tax payers.

- Property taxation will be revised in connection with the real estate registration system. Currently the property tax applies only to dwellings and boats not used for business purposes. The taxable base should be widened to include all types of immovable property, regardless of location (eg rural), and including those used for business purposes.

The Slovenian tax system is fairly well harmonized with all EU tax directives with the exception of the three above-mentioned directives relating to corporate income tax. In the case of the first two, currently there is no specific tax treatment beyond national borders. Therefore, special laws would have to be introduced at the time Slovenia joins the EU. Concerning the third directive, there is no such tax in Slovenia and consideration is currently being given to whether or not to introduce it.

Besides the harmonization of the tax system with that in EU countries, the tax policy is also committed to the same goals pursued by the EU. From this perspective, and consistent with WTO rules, the requirement for preferential tax treatment in the Special Economic Zone that 51 per cent of the turnover produced must be exported should be abrogated.

3.4

Financial Support and Finance Facilities from the EU

Bank Austria Creditanstalt

The Accession Partnerships and their operation

The EU makes available some EUR 3 billion annually to ensure that the appropriate flanking measures accompany the accession process. This substantial financial assistance is intended to be used for drawing up tailor-made plans to assist the countries in preparing for accession. However, the actual investments required of the candidates are many times greater.

The budgetary basis for the EU programme is the Agenda 2000, which sets the financial framework for the EU for the years 2000 to 2006. Accession Partnerships are drawn up annually for each accession candidate to define its short-term, medium-term and long-term goals which also include the major financial assistance being granted, so that they are the core element of European assistance for enlargement. Each Accession Partnership is supplemented by a National Programme for the Adoption of the Acquis (NPAA) produced by the accession candidate in which the concrete actions they plan to take to achieve the goals set down in the Accession Partnership are stated. On this basis, the EC signs what is known as a Financial Memorandum every year with each individual accession candidate. This memorandum contains the projects and programmes which are to be co-funded by the EU.

Following accession to the EU, assistance will be based on European regional policy directives and regulations, and the programmes of the Structured Funds and the Cohesion Fund will apply from the negotiated accession dates.

Presumably, most accession regimes will be classified as Objective 1 regions (regions whose development is lagging behind). At present, some

70 per cent of European assistance goes to Objective 1 regions. Therefore, unless the EU decides to exceed greatly the budget fixed for the period up to 2006, the successful accession candidates will initially receive only a certain percentage of the possible funding assistance. Sufficient assurance must also be given that each country has adequate administrative capacity to implement the European assistance policy and to monitor efficiently the use of resources.

EU budgetary issues

The Commission's plan has diverged from the Agenda 2000 concluded in March 1999 in two respects: the first countries will join the EU in 2004 at the very earliest (instead of 2002) and the number of first-wave accessions is now assumed to be ten instead of the original six.

Prior to the Copenhagen conference, obligations in the EU budget towards accession candidates were set at EUR 10.8 billion (2004), with increases to EUR 13.4 billion (2005) and EUR 16 billion (2006). Specific provisions were earmarked within the overall budget for agriculture, possibly the most divisive issue in the accession negotiations, structural policy and 'internal policies' such as nuclear safety.

In the case of agriculture, the allocation to market measures of the common agricultural policy (CAP) is EUR 516 million. In its draft report, following discussion at the Berlin summit, the Commission foresaw a two-phase model according to which direct payments will be gradually increased until they match the level of support which is generally applicable to all member states of the EU in 2013. A second area in the chapter on agriculture concerns rural development in relation to managing the effects of the CAP. The financial resources assigned to this area would amount to EUR 1,532 million in 2004, rising to 1,781 million by 2006. One-third of these funds could be provided through the Cohesion Fund, with the advantage that the co-financing by the EU would amount to 85 per cent instead of 80 per cent.

Structural policy is the second major expense area. The subsidies granted to the new member states are massive compared to their per capita GDP, which is low by EU standards. The Commission proposes that funds amounting to EUR 7,067 million be made available to the new member states in 2004, increasing to EUR 8,150 million in 2005 and to EUR 10,350 million in 2006.

A further area of support is the building of institutions, referred to above, but these funds will be reduced after accession. A total of about EUR 1 billion is currently being made available, mostly under the PHARE programme, to the candidate countries for the development of their administrative systems and for taking over the *acquis communautaire*.

The overall financial framework for enlargement for the period 2004 to 2006 is summarized in Table 3.4.1.

Difficult negotiation issues

Table 3.4.1 Financial framework for enlargement, 2004–2006 (€ million, 1999 prices)

	2004	2005	2006
Commitment appropriations	2048	3596	3923
Structural actions	7067	8150	10,350
Internal policies	1176	1096	1071
Administration	503	558	612
Total commitment appropriations	10,794	13,400	15,966
Total commitment appropriations (Berlin 1999 scenario)	11,610	14,200	16,760
Payment appropriations (Enlargement)	5,686	10,493	11,840
Payment appropriations (Berlin 1999 scenario)	8,890	11,440	14,220

1) Scenario: Accession of 10 New Member States in 2004
Source: European Commission

Agriculture

The number of persons employed in the agricultural sector and the relevant share of GDP are much higher in the candidate countries than in the EU. However, employment in Slovenia in the agri-food industry is 9.9 per cent, in contrast to Poland where agricultural employment is highest at 25.7 per cent, but is more than twice that of the Czech Republic (4.8 per cent).

Contributory factors in the significance of the agricultural sector in the CEE have been motives such as self-sufficiency in food production and the high subsidies received by the sector generally in the region. Whatever the reasons, the impact of the CAP will be considerable.

Unemployment in Slovenia has declined steadily since 1999, although GDP has also decreased each year since 1999, except for 2002 when it recovered slightly. Agriculture is just one of the sectors where increased productivity has not contributed to the reduction in unemployment.

Direct payments

Among the measures agreed at the 1999 Berlin summit for the reform of the CAP were a reduction of intervention prices, with the objective of moving from price subsidies to direct payments. The lowering of intervention prices, which reduces income, was offset by higher direct payments. As the agricultural prices in the candidate countries in the CEE are also partly below the intervention prices, this measure would amount to an additional price subsidy. The efforts of recent years to establish a competitive agricultural system in the CEE, which were supported by the EU, would be countered or at least delayed from a prompt and complete outcome by taking over the system of direct payments. Not only would the present structure become more inflexible, new tensions would also result as incomes in the agricultural sector would rise to well above those of an industrial worker. For this reason the Commission called for a plan to be implemented gradually by stages. However, at present France and Germany, while insisting on imposing a cap on overall farm spending in Europe, have combined to block any general reform of the CAP.

Financial support from the EU for accession candidates

The European Commission has tasked itself to provide a comprehensive finance package to help the 10 accession candidates (Cyprus, Czech Republic, Estonia, Hungary, Latvia, Lithuania, Malta, Poland, Slovak Republic and Slovenia) prepare for accession to the EU. The support is being provided through three programmes from 2000 to 2006: PHARE, ISPA and SAPARD. The total annual budget of about EUR 3 billion for the three initiatives is allocated as EUR 1.5 billion for PHARE, EUR 1 billion for ISPA and EUR 0.5 billion for SAPARD.

PHARE

The PHARE programme takes the form of non-repayable grants from the EC to support goals set in the Accession Partnerships to prepare candidates for EU accession. There are two main priorities: 1) investment support to help the accession candidates adapt their infrastructure and enterprises and bring them up to EU standards – 70 per cent of PHARE is allocated to meeting this goal; 2) institution-building – 30 per cent of the budget is allocated to the goal of developing and strengthening institutions so that the candidate is equipped to adopt and implement the EU legal system with the necessary administrative resources.

PHARE programmes are no longer based on demand from the individual countries but exclusively on the needs arising from the forthcoming accession. General programmes for the environment, transportation infrastructure and agriculture are no longer included. A number of needs-oriented programmes have been created for each accession candidate on the basis of the Accession Partnership and the ensuing Financing Memorandum. The EC has set up a separate Internet page for each country and sector: http://europa.eu.int/phare-cgi/plsql/prog.search.

Like ISPA and SAPARD (see below), the PHARE programme is implemented in a decentralized manner, ie the recipient countries are responsible for programme execution. In most projects funded by PHARE, the companies which are to carry out the projects are determined in international tendering procedures. Forecast tenders are published by the EC's office for external aid programmes, Europ-Aid Co-operation Office, on the following Internet page: http://europa.eu.int/comm/europeaid/cgi/frame12.pl.

Companies and experts wishing to participate in the public tenders should first enter their names in the central Consultant Register, which serves as the central database for the European Commission. Based on the project information provided on the Internet, companies can register their interest by sending a 'letter of interest'. If the company is put on the 'shortlist', it can participate in the actual public tender.

National programmes

A large part of PHARE funds goes to national programmes negotiated by the EC and the accession candidates on the basis of the Accession Partnerships. These programmes include schemes promoting cross-border cooperation with neighbouring countries.

Individual projects are drawn up on the basis of the national programmes. The final report containing key statements and information on a project can be obtained from the Delegation of the European Commission in the country concerned.

Delegation of the European Commission
Slovenia
Trg. Republike 3/XI
SLO-1000 Ljubljana
Tel: (+386 1) 252 88 00
Fax: (+386 1) 425 20 85
E-mail: delegation-slovenia@cec.eu.int

Multi-beneficiary programmes

Most of the remaining funds go to horizontal and cross-border initiatives tailored not to a single country, as are the national programmes, but to promoting a given sector or topic. They apply equally to all accession candidates and are administered by the EC in cooperation with the countries involved. The EC is reducing programmes which do not provide assistance tailored to accession as a part of the realignment of PHARE. Existing programmes can be found on Internet page: http://europa.eu.int/comm/enlargement/pas/phare/programmes/multi-bene/index.htm.

Opening up of EU programmes to accession candidates
Since 1998, successive steps have been taken to open up sectoral programmes open to all EU member states to the accession candidates as well. An overview of the EU programmes in which Slovakia participates is presented on the following Internet page: http://europa.eu.int/comm/enlargement/pas/ocp_index.htm.

ISPA

Since the beginning of 2000, an annual EUR 1,040 million in structural assistance has been made available to EU accession candidates through the Instrument for Structural Policies for Pre-Accession (ISPA). The funds are directed to three areas:

- *Environment* – to bring accession candidates up to EU environmental standards, with a focus on areas involving heavy costs, ie drinking water supply, waste-water treatment and air pollution and solid-waste management.

- *Transport* – with the goal of improving the mobility of people and the transport of goods through investment in infrastructure, particularly in relation to the development of the Trans-European networks (TEN).

- *Technical assistance* – a minor part of the budget is used to fund feasibility studies and project management. (There is a similar PHARE Programme).

Financial assistance can cover up to 75 per cent, in special cases up to 85 per cent, of project costs; projects should involve a minimum investment of EUR 5 million. Co-financing arrangements can be entered into with international finance institutions (IFIs) or with commercial banks. Project selection and monitoring is carried out by the EC.

There are current provisions for annual assistance of EUR 5 million under ISPA for Slovenia, of which details may found on Internet page: http://europa.eu.int/comm/regional_policy/funds/ispa_en.htm.

Companies planning to carry out projects in the accession candidate countries with PHARE or ISPA assistance are advised to contact the office administering the relevant programme at an early stage to discuss potential inclusion of that project. A list of contacts for ISPA and the PHARE Address Book are readily available from the Bank Austria Creditanstalt Group's EU Advisory team identified in Appendix 2.

SAPARD

The Special Accession Programme for Agriculture and Rural Development (SAPARD) came into effect at the beginning of 2000 and is intended to:

- promote sustainable rural development;

- resolve the problems related to the long-term adaptation of the agricultural sector and rural areas;

- support the accession candidate countries in adopting and implementing the *acquis communautaire* in the area of the CAP and related measures.

Priorities vary considerably from country to country. Overall under SAPARD, more than EUR 500 million annually is made available. The funds allocated differ considerably among the individual countries.

A SAPARD agency has been set up in each country to agree the projects to be selected and administer a Multi-annual Financing Agreement with the EU as a master agreement for the priorities to be financed. The maximum project size varies from country to country and an Annual Financing Agreement is signed determining the amount to be committed for each year. SAPARD funds take the form of non-repayable grants up to a maximum of 50 per cent of project costs and are advanced to enterprises, individuals and, in certain cases, government agencies in the agricultural sector of candidate countries. Beneficiaries are responsible for raising the remaining funds.

SAPARD differs from other external aid programmes of the EC in that projects must be filed directly with the SAPARD agency in the relevant country.

Further information about SAPARD is available from the following Internet page: http://europa.eu.int/comm/agriculture/external/enlarge/index_en.htm.

EU SME Finance Facility Phase II (SME FF)

In addition to the three basic aid programmes, the EU Commission launched a regional Finance Facility in 1999 for the 10 applicant countries. The EC administers the programme in cooperation with the EBRD, the EIB and the Council of Europe Development Bank (CEB) or KfW (Kreditanstalt für Wiederaufbau). The Facility is funded from PHARE resources.

The essential purpose of the programme is to facilitate long-term lending to small and medium-sized enterprises (SMEs) by local financial institutions (banks and equity funds) in the applicant countries. Support is extended to these intermediaries in two ways: the 'traditional' lending procedure through the so-called 'Loan and Guarantee Window'; and the 'Equity Window', whereby the EBRD makes available equity capital and management support. The final borrowers, local SMEs, have to meet certain minimum local and national standards in the areas of environmental protection, security and health protection.

Bank Austria Creditanstalt Slovenia (http://www.ba-ca.si) has signed agreements for refinancing lines with EIB and, since 2001, with KfW, covering a total amount of EUR 70 million. The funds may be used by SMEs, and also by territorial authorities, PPPs and companies active in promoting the interests of communities, for infrastructure projects. These refinancing lines are a pre-condition for participation in the 'Loan Window' of the EU SME Finance Facility. Bank Austria Creditanstalt Slovenija is currently negotiating participation in this programme.

In Slovenia, SME FF arrangements currently exist with the Slovene Export Corporation, and in the Equity Window with Bank Koper d.d. and Nova Kreditna Banka maribor d.d.

The content of this chapter is a consolidation of papers from the Bank Austria Creditanstalt Economics Department publications: 'Investment Guide on Slovenia', July 2002, East–West Report 4/2002 and CEE Report 3-2003.

Part Four

Key Sectors of Industry and Business

4.1

Agriculture and Food Industries

Dr Roman Glaser, CEO Perutnina Ptuj, and Jani Toros, Marketing Manager Mlinotest

Introduction

Slovenia is a small country with a population of only about 2 million people. However, its geographical position is very important; the crossroads of Germanic, Romanic and Balkan cultures creates a rich basis for culinary experiments. Throughout culinary history and today, people have mixed the best of the three cultures and created a delicious traditional Slovenian kitchen. Despite ongoing polemical discussions about what is the real and genuine Slovenian food, the fact remains unchanged – Slovenians always eat delicious and tasty food.

Home gardening and food growing are very popular in Slovenia. Small private vegetable and fruit gardens are very common in suburban parts of the country. Home-grown, produced and cooked food is completely natural, without artificial additives. Herbs play an important role in the Slovenian kitchen. Many people grow herbs in pots on window sills and balconies. Relatives who live in the countryside often bring fresh and home-grown food supplies to their urban families. The start of winter is a time for 'meat and sausage days', when families' deep freezers are loaded with home and naturally bred meats.

These habits are becoming rare with the increasing tempo of modern life. The importance of naturally grown foods remains in people's minds, so Slovenians expect healthy and tasty products from the modern food industry.

Slovenia is a country with a huge potential in naturally grown foods. The Slovenian food processing industry manages some important and very well-known product brands.

Agriculture

According to the 2000 census, Slovenia had 86,336 private farms and 131 agricultural companies. The average size of a farm grew from 4.1 to 5.3 hectares between 1991 and 2000, with an increasing number of farms larger than 10 hectares and a decreasing number of farms with 1–10 hectares.

The vegetable harvest contributes about 30 per cent to the net agricultural harvest (approx. 14 per cent agronomy and 7 per cent fruit growing and viniculture). The sowing structure has remained stable throughout the years, with 58 per cent being cereals (mainly corn for grain and wheat), followed by silage corn and other green fodders (total of 27 per cent). Sugar beet and potatoes also represent a fair share. Total acreage of permanent plantations has remained stable over the years, with a prevailing share being taken up by vineyards.

Stockbreeding represents 70 per cent net of agriculture and is therefore important for Slovenian agriculture. Almost 90 per cent of all farmhouses breed livestock and about 77 per cent of livestock is cattle. The number of dairy cows is in decline, but milk production is growing due to breeding concentration and specialization. Pigs represent over 12 per cent of livestock and the rest are horses, sheep, goats, rabbits, poultry and others.

Slovenia is a traditional importer of agricultural products because domestic agricultural production is not adequate. Agricultural share in the total foreign trade deficit fell from 70 per cent in 1994 to 36 per cent in 2001. Foreign trade with agricultural products represented about 3.7 per cent of total Slovenian material exports and 6.6 per cent of total material imports.

Slovenia's major agricultural trading partners are the EU, CEFTA and the former Yugoslavian countries. The majority of Slovenian agricultural products are imported from the EU and exported to the countries of the former Yugoslavia. Agricultural trade used to be very limited in the past, but now Slovenia has different international arrangements that have opened borders to agricultural trading and caused price pressure on the domestic market. In the first decade after Slovenian independence (in 1991) prices of agricultural products were very unstable among different manufacturers. Prices grew faster than total inflation in 1992, but dropped significantly the year after. They started to grow again between 1994 and 1996 because of government protection and price control. Between 1996 and the end of 2000 prices dropped again and fell behind national averages. In 2001 agricultural products prices rose again. See Table 4.1.1.

Food processing industry

High-quality, healthy and safe domestic food products are one of Slovenia's major competitive advantages. Slovenia, with its highly

Table 4.1.1 Added value and gross domestic product (GDP) in agriculture, fishing industry and forestry

	1992	1993	1994	1995	1996	1997	1998	1999	2000	2001
Added value, current prices (in million SIT) agriculture, fishing	52.634	64.492	73.150	87.072	98.260	107.700	116.215	114.552	115.101	124.161
industry and forestry	246	224	239	386	439	484	519	520	534	460
Real added value yearly	−6.6	−4.1	4.2	1.6	1.0	−2.9	3.1	−2.1	−1.0	−2.1
growth agriculture, fishing industry and forestry	−19.0	−37.0	5.2	−6.1	9.6	1.7	−4.4	3.1	−3.5	1.3
Share of total added value in % agriculture, fishing industry and forestry	5.9	5.2	4.6	4.6	4.5	4.3	4.2	3.7	3.3	3.1
Share of total GDP in % agriculture, fishing industry and forestry	5.2	4.5	4.0	3.9	3.9	3.7	3.6	3.2	2.9	2.7

Source: SURS (Statisticne informacije, st. 103/2002), calculations of Institute of Macroeconomic Analysis and Development UMAR

developed ecological awareness, is an ideal place for a natural food chain from the field to the fork. Slovenia is not a country with a huge agricultural industry, but it has a strong and developed food-processing industry. Agriculture plays an important role in the natural development of the state, regional identity and in the relationship between strategic regional and social factors. Agriculture represents 2.7 per cent of Slovenian GDP, but its combination with different factors contributes to 70 per cent of Slovenian food self-sufficiency. The superiority of the Slovenian agriculture and food-processing industry guarantees its customers a natural, healthy, fresh and *not* genetically modified food. This is the direction of the food-processing industry in Slovenia now and in the days to come.

The majority of Slovenian food-processing companies have merged with multinational corporations; however, there are some cases where they have not. Tables 4.1.2, 4.1.3 and 4.1.4 show Slovenian food-processing industry trends.

Slovenian macroeconomic conditions benefit the agronomical, agricultural and food-processing industry. Slovenian GDP will increase from the current SIT 4,500 billion to SIT 5,700 billion in the next couple of years. Inflation will decrease to 3.2 per cent and other macroeconomic advantages will increase the economic stability of Slovenia. This way Slovenia will be in a better macroeconomic position than many current EU members even before entering the EU (on 1 May 2004). Dynamic development and equilibration of demand and supply indicate an increase of Slovenian exports as well as the import of products and services in the future.

Table 4.1.2 Trends of major economic indicators in Slovenian food-processing industry 1998–2002

	1998	1999	2000	2001	2002	Index 2001/2002	Index 2002/1998
No. of enterprises	368	383	388	377	394	104.5	107.1
No. of employees	18.038	19.724	19.473	19.281	19.841	102.9	110.0
Turnover (billion SIT)	293.9	326.4	355.4	391.1	418.3	99.5	105.7
Export sales (billion SIT)	42.8	51.5	62.1	74.1	76.6	96.1	132.8
Productivity (000 SIT)	16.292	16.546	18.252	20.284	21.083	96.7	96.1
Value added / empl. (000 SIT)	4.497	4.736	5.105	5.450	5.910	100.9	97.6
Net profit /empl. (000 SIT)	619.6	656.9	241.6	72	503.4	650.4	60.3

Source: University of Ljubljana – Zootechnical Department Chair for Agricultural Economics, Policy and Law

Table 4.1.3 Structural share of Slovenian food-processing industry (DA; NACE) in total processing industry (D–NACE)

	DA share in D (D = 100)					Index 2002/2001	Index 2002/1998
	1998	1999	2000	2001	2002		
No. of enterprises	5.89	6.10	6.21	6.1	6.17	101.1	104.6
No. of employees	8.53	9.32	9.22	9.09	9.14	100.6	107.2
Turnover	12.22	12.69	11.57	11.26	10.98	97.5	89.9
Value added	11.86	11.18	10.81	10.7	10.3	96.4	87.0
Profit	17.25	14.41	11.25	10.85	11.7	107.5	67.6
Loss	5.16	4.87	17.92	19.65	16.4	83.3	317.3
Export sales	3.32	3.81	3.61	3.74	3.58	103.1	107.7

Source: University of Ljubljana – Zootechnical Department Chair for Agricultural Economics, Policy and Law

Slovenia has positioned itself as a medium-developed national region within Europe. According to the Slovenian macro-economist, Dr Kovac, Slovenia's restructuring has to result in at least five Slovenian-based multinational corporations, 200 large national companies and 2,000 fast-growing small businesses being successful and competitive in national and international markets. National privatization is pretty much over. The government is managing only limited and unique resources. Agricultural lands are owned by the National Fund of Agricultural Lands and are managed by agricultural companies based on long-term lease contracts.

The Slovenian food products export structure is leaning towards the former Yugoslavian countries, but exports to the EU increased last year

Table 4.1.4 Structure of Slovenian food-processing industry in 2002

Activity	No. of enterprises	No. of employees	Turnover sales	Export added	Value loss	Net profit/ (billon SIT)
	Structure in % (Total food industry = 100 %)					
15.1 Meat-processing industry	17.5	28.3	23.9	12.1	19.8	−2.844.0
15.2 Fish-processing industry	1.8	1.3	0.9	1.8	1.1	336.9
15.3 Fruit and vegetable processing industry	9.1	9.7	11.3	23.4	10.9	1.409.5
15.4 Production of oils and fats	1.8	1.0	1.9	1.9	1.1	−74.9
15.5 Dairy industry	5.8	8.9	15.2	13.0	9.2	1.219.6
15.6 Milling industry	3.3	4.4	4.6	4.9	4.2	558.7
15.7 Animal feed production	2.0	0.3	0.4	0.0	0.2	10.5
15.81 Bakery	28.9	21.4	12.3	1.5	17.1	1.131.6
15.83 Sugar processing	0.3	1.3	1.9	0.1	2.4	862.8
15.84 Confectionery	1.5	3.7	2.4	4.8	2.7	193.0
15.86 Tea and coffee processing	6.1	4.0	5.1	9.0	6.3	1.498.2
15.93 Vine production	3.6	4.4	2.9	1.9	3.0	−355.7
15.96 Brewery	2.3	5.1	8.7	13.9	10.1	2.054.8
15.98 Production of non-alcoholic beverages	3.3	3.2	3.4	3.9	4.4	−354.6
16. Tobacco industry	0.3	1.6	4.1	7.0	6.1	3.982.9
Other food-processing activities	12.4	1.4	1.0	0.8	1.4	359.7

Source: University of Ljubljana – Zootechnical Department Chair for Agricultural Economics, Policy and Law

(Figure 4.1.1). It is expected that this trend will continue and that exports to the EU will increase even more after Slovenia becomes a fully authorized member of the EU in May 2004.

An overview of the import–export structure shows us that the majority of Slovenian exports in 2002 were beer, non-alcoholic beverages and dairy products (Figure 4.1.2). Imports that same year consisted of animal oils and fats, fruit and vegetables (Figure 4.1.3). The level of imports and exports of meat and fish products was about the same in 2002.

When Slovenia enters the EU the import–export laws and conditions will change and the current structure will most probably change.

Where do we go from here?

Slovenian strategic potential is definitely not in the mass production of low-priced products. The country has a huge potential in the agriculture and food-processing industries with production of high-quality products in low quantities to satisfy a demanding customer who is looking for

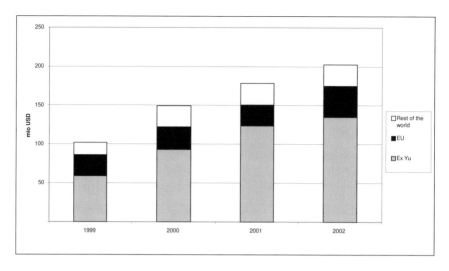

Source: University of Ljubljana – Zootechnical Department Chair for Agricultural Economics, Policy and Law

Figure 4.1.1 Structure of Slovenian export of processed food products by destination in 2002

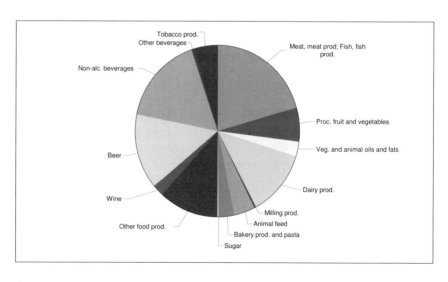

Source: University of Ljubljana – Zootechnical Department Chair for Agricultural Economics, Policy and Law

Figure 4.1.2 Structure of Slovenian exports of processed food products in 2002

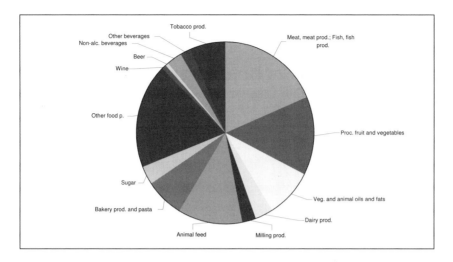

Source: University of Ljubljana – Zootechnical Department Chair for Agricultural Economics, Policy and Law

Figure 4.1.3 Structure of Slovenian imports of processed food products in 2002

healthy and tasty food. Limited resources, national specialities and biological food production are the main potentials of the Slovenian agriculture and food-processing industries.

4.2

Forestry, Forest Products and Wood Processing

Jonathan Reuvid

Forestry

Many forests have been created in Slovenia's moderate climatic conditions due to the overgrowing of agricultural land. Slovenian forests are relatively well preserved in this region of varied terrain and diverse geological conditions. There is a wide variety of tree species, as Table 4.2.1 demonstrates.

Table 4.2.1 Tree species composition in % of total growing stock

	%
Norway spruce	33
Beech	32
Silver fir	8
Oak species	7
Pine species	6
Noble broadleaves	4
Other broadleaves	9
Other conifers	1
	100

Source: Ministry of Agriculture, Forestry and Food

The ownership of private property in Slovenia is fragmented, with about 350,000 forest owners having an average of 2.3 hectares divided into smaller spatial units. Forests are of little economic significance to small-scale forest owners, who generally lack suitable qualifications to undertake forest work.

Indeed, the share of forestry in the Slovenian economy has never been significant and continues to decrease, which is a characteristic trend in all developed countries. The industry's present contribution to GDP is less than 0.5 per cent.

Yet, on the other hand, more than half of Slovenia's surface is covered with forests, which provides forestry with an altogether different dimension that certainly cannot be measured by its contribution to GDP. Sustainability, close-to-nature management and multi-functionality are the guiding principles of forest management in Slovenia. The use of small-scale forest management measures which take into account natural site conditions and the natural process in forest development is explicit. The bio-ecological and economic stability of forests is enhanced by these means.

General statistics on the development of forests and forestry in Slovenia are summarized in Table 4.2.2.

Table 4.2.2 The evolution of forests and forestry in Slovenia

	1900	1950	1970	1980	1990	2000
Forest area (000 ha)	737	860	1008	1027	1077	1143
Growing stock (m³/ha)	–	126	175	185	192	234
Private forests (%)	–	68	63	64	62	71
Average annual felling (000 m³)	–	2860	3141	3318	2274	2300

Source: Ministry of Agriculture, Forests and Food

The potential felling in forest management plans has been set at the level of 57 per cent of increment in conifers and 46 per cent in broad-leaved species. However, a discrepancy between potential and actual felling is recorded every year, particularly in private forests, indicating that small-scale forest owners rely little on forest income. Actual felling in 2000 amounted to 75 per cent of the potential felling (81 per cent in conifers, 69 per cent in broad-leaved species).

Industry organization

There are approximately 160 companies and independent entrepreneurs engaged in the Slovenian forest industry, of which 15 have been granted concessions to exploit state-owned forests. They represent by far the largest share of forestry activity. There are 6 large and 13 medium-sized companies operating in the field; the remaining operators are small companies.

Forestry companies mainly perform the following services:

● felling and harvesting of wood;

● performance of silvicultural and protection work in forests;

- building and maintenance of forest roads and trails;

- transport of wood;

- purchase of wood and sawn wood from privately owned forests;

- horticulture;

- wood processing.

The main forestry products offered by forestry companies are:

- logs for sawmills;

- technical wood;

- wood for chemical processing and firewood;

- primary wood processing products (sawn wood, wood panels, roofing, etc);

- biomass for heating purposes.

Some companies are additionally engaged in hunting, their main offering including the organization and realization of hunting for breeding and tourist-recreational purposes and the selling of game.

Forestry company performance

The industry employs about 2,000 workers. The analysis in Table 4.2.3 has been drawn from the financial accounts of the 15 largest companies.

Table 4.2.3 Major forestry company performance

	SIT 000	% share in economy
Income – total	17,024,198	0.19
Net income from domestic sales	13,229,408	0.22
Net income from foreign sales	2,494,153	0.11

Comparing the financial indicators of these companies with those of the wood-processing industry, which is the most closely related industry, those of the building industry (similarly labour-intensive) and even the economy, it is clear that the forestry companies perform better. They have a large degree of financial independence and their indebtedness is low.

Salaries and labour costs are generally higher, while profit per employee is lower. The value added per employee in comparison with the wood-processing and building industries is higher, yet still below the average of the economy as a whole.

The forestry companies' share of foreign sales is also less, which reflects the nature of the products and services offered. There are hardly any foreign investments in Slovenian forestry; conversely, the industry does not make foreign investments itself.

Wood-processing industry

The wood-processing industry employed approximately 21,000 workers in 2001, engaged primarily in the processing of treatment and wood and the manufacture of furniture. The total revenue generated by the industry that year was approximately SIT 226.8 billion. Average value added per employee in 2001 amounted to EUR 14,560. In relation to the economy as a whole, the wood-processing industry employed 4.4 per cent of the workforce in 2.5 per cent of the total number of companies.

The wood-processing industry is a net exporter, with direct and indirect exports in 2001 amounting to USD 993.6 million and imports to USD 348.1 million. The top 10 export destinations, in descending order, are Germany, Italy, Croatia, Austria, the USA, France, Great Britain, Belgium, Bosnia and Hercegovina, and Yugoslavia and the top 10 sources of imports are Italy, Germany, Austria, Croatia, France, China, Poland, Bosnia and Hercegovina, the Czech Republic and Slovakia.

4.3

The Energy Sector

TIPO

Energy requirements and sources

Slovenia is highly dependent on energy imports, having only limited domestic energy sources. Up to 2000, energy dependence was running at 73 to 75 per cent, but it rose to 76.8 per cent in 2001 as a result of a reduction in domestic coal mining. In other words, domestic resources satisfied only 23.2 per cent of demand, estimated at 296.5 penta joules (PJ) of primary energy, in 2001, with increased usage of imported natural gas, oil derivatives and nuclear fuels accounting for the balance. EU resources provide 50.5 per cent of the primary energy demand.

Among the domestic sources of primary energy are the hydro power of Slovenian rivers, which satisfies 4.5 per cent of primary usage, and solid fuels, especially lignite and brown coal, which account for a further 16 per cent of primary usage. Table 4.3.1 defines the primary energy resources required in 2001.

Table 4.3.1 Primary energy requirements 2001

	%
Crude oil	37.0
Solid fuels	22.7
Nuclear fuels	19.0
Natural gas	12.7
Hydro power	4.4
Firewood and wood waste	4.0
New resources	0.2

In terms of final usage, ie the energy supplied to consumers, electric power accounts for a 20 per cent share and solid fuels for an 8.3 per cent share of the total. Within the electric power industry, hydro power plants represent nearly one-third of total production. Similar shares of slightly more than one-third each of electric power are generated by coal-fired thermal plants and by nuclear power plants.

The Slovenian per capita consumption amounts to 3.61 tons of crude oil equivalent, compared to 3.91 tons average among EU member states and 8.22 tons in the USA.

In total, energy usage in Slovenia represents only about half a per cent of the EU's total energy usage. Throughout the period since independence the energy supply to Slovenia has remained reliable and stable, both in the supply of crude oil derivatives and natural gas, in coal and in the long-distance supply of heat and electric power.

Market usage and local energy production industry

Motor fuel standards for Slovenia have been harmonized with EU standards and the quality of Slovenian energy supply is comparable to that of the EU countries. The natural gas network has been connected with sources from Algeria and Russia and the electric-power system is integrated with the European interconnection UCTE.

In 2000, all Slovenian activities comprising motor fuel supply together generated a 9.33 per cent share in total revenues of the entire Slovenian economy, although employment in this sector represents a mere 3.4 per cent of all workers employed.

The highest value added per employee was achieved by the electrical generation industry at EUR 47,500, followed by the gaseous fuels supply sector with EUR 44,500 and liquid fuels supply with nearly EUR 36,000.

Slovenia's estimated usage of final energy in 2001 was 189 PJ. Table 4.3.2 identifies the usage by sector.

Table 4.3.2 2001 usage of final energy by sector

	%
Liquid fuels	51
Electric power	21
Gaseous fuels	16
Solid fuels	8
District heating	4

The estimated usage of energy for 2001 in the field of traffic is 32 per cent of total usage, it is 28 per cent in the field of industry and the balance of 40 per cent is in all other categories. The usage of final energy in Slovenia peaked in 1987 at 167.3 PJ, before dropping to its lowest level in 1992 with 150 PJ. Two major influences in the steadily increasing usage of final energy since 1992 have been usage efficiency and the intensive introduction of natural gas in supplies to local communities.

In recent years, international energy markets throughout Europe have undergone great changes with the opening of national markets in the fields of electricity and natural gas supply, while prices of oil and its derivatives have run wild. Slovenia adapted to these new circumstances by enacting in September 1999 the Energy Act, which harmonized the supply of electric power and natural gas in Slovenia with the EU directives and requirements of the European Energy Charter.

On 15 April 2002, the Slovenian power market was opened to internal competition and it was further opened to external competition in 2003. Consumers with an installed capacity of more than 41 kW can now be supplied with electric power from foreign suppliers.

In accordance with the agreements reached with Croatia on the unresolved questions concerning its operation, the Krsko nuclear power plant now supplies half of its generated electric power to Croatia.

The Slovenian natural gas market has also been opened, as envisaged by the Energy Act 1999, in a series of steps. From 1 January 2003, the gas market was opened for consumers with a yearly consumption exceeding 25 million m³. The open market will be extended to consumers with an annual consumption of 5 million m³ or more from 1 January 2008.

Pricing of energy and fuels

The model for the pricing of oil derivatives in current use enables a prompt adjustment of petrol prices to both crude oil price movements and the US dollar exchange rate. Likewise, the pricing model for natural gas from the main network enables a prompt adjustment to price movements on international markets. Both models have re-established order in the pricing field, which used to be governmentally regulated.

The Slovenian government has passed a decree on the pricing of steam and hot water used for purposes of district heating on the basis of a methodology for determining and monitoring district heating prices commissioned by communal energy companies. Under this decree a pricing mechanism was determined which replaced the former lengthy price change procedures.

The price regulations are of great importance, particularly in periods of rapid change and increases in imported fuel prices, characteristic of the period from 2000.

Major energy enterprises by activity

Coal mining

● Rudnik lignita Velenje. Partizanska cesta 78, 3320 Velenje

● Rudnik Trbovlje Hrastnik. Trg revolucije 14, 1420 Trbovlje

Nuclear power production

● Rudnik Zirovski vrh (winding down). Todrasz 1, 4224 Gorenja vas

Oil and gas production

● Petrol, Slovenska naftna druszba, d.d. Dunajska 50, 1000 Ljubljana

● Istrabenz d.d. Ferrarska 7, 6000 Koper

● Geoplin d.d. Ulica ljubljanske brigade 11a, 1000 Ljubljana

● Nafta lendava, d.o.o. Rudaska 1, 9220 Lendava

● Adriaplin Ljubljana. Cesta ljubljanske brigade 11, 1000 Ljubljana

● Apegas Ljubljana. Linhartova cesta 3/A, 1000 Ljubljana

● Plinarna Maribor d.d. Plinarniska ulica 9, 2000 Ljubljana

● Mestni plinovodi d.o.o. Koper Kolodvorska cesta 2, 6000 Koper

● Mapetrol d.o.o. Linhartova ulica 17A, 2000 Maribor

Electricity supply

● Nuklearna elektrarna Krsko. Production of NE, Vrbina 12, 8270 Krsko

● Dravske elektrarne Maribor. Production of HE, Obrezna 170, 2000 Maribor

● Savske elektrarne Ljubljana. Production of HE, Hajdrihova 2, 1000 Ljubljana

● Soske elektrarne Nova Gorica. Production of HE, Erjaveeva 20, 5000 Nova Gorica

● Termoelektrarne Sostanj. Production of TE, Lola Ribarja 18, 3325 Sostanj

● Termoelektrarna Trbovlje. Production of TE, Obzeleznici 3, 1420 Trbovlje

- Termoelektrarna toplarna Ljubljarna. Production of TE, Toplkanriska 19, 1000 Ljubljana

- Elektrarna Brestanica. Production of TE, Cesta prvih borcev 18, 8280 Brestanica

- Elektro Slovenija. Elec. Transmission, Hajdrihova 2, 1000 Ljubljana

- Elektro Celjie. Distribution, Vruneeva 2a, 3000 Celje

- Elektro Gorenjska. Distribution, Bleiwesova 6, 4000 Kranj

- Elektro Ljubljana. Distribution, Slovenska cesta 58, 1000 Ljubljana

- Elektro Maribor. Distribution, Vetrinjska 2, 2000 Maribor

- Elektro Primorska. Distribution, Erjaveeva 22, 5000 Nova Gorica

4.4

Building Materials Industry

TIPO

The building materials industry is an important activity within the Slovenian construction sector in terms of the quantity and value of materials needed for infrastructure and the construction of buildings. The industry consists of manufactures of lime, cement and cement products, bricks and roofing tiles, semi-finished construction products, stone and various types of insulation materials.

In 2000 the total annual value of building materials reached SIT 62.9 billion, 2.2 per cent less in real terms than in 1996, although 6.7 per cent more in monetary value. The breakdown of 2000 production is detailed in Table 4.4.1 and compared with 1996.

Table 4.4.1 Value of building materials production in 2000

	Net sales SIT billion	Index (1996 = 100)
Quarrying of stone for construction purposes, quarrying of sand and clay	5.7	97.3
Manufacture of tiles, bricks and other ceramic products for construction	8.5	107.0
Production of cement	16.2	108.9
Production of lime	2.5	94.3
Manufacture of concrete, cement and plaster products	24.3	108.2
Machining of natural stone	5.7	102.4
Total	62.9	106.7

Source: Construction and Building Materials Association, Slovenia

There are 154 companies engaged in the Slovenian building materials industry, of which 14 are classified as large and 25 as medium-sized companies. The total industry workforce is reported as 4,191 people.

The non-metallic mineral products industry, comprising extraction and production activities of which the building materials are a part, employed 5,581 workers in 2000, accounting for 2.6 per cent of the workforce.

Industry performance

Slovenia is a net exporter of building materials. In 2000, the export activities of Slovenian companies generated SIT 6.7 billion, while imports of more than SIT 5 billion were registered. The composition of exports by product groups is detailed in Table 4.4.2.

Table 4.4.2 Export of building materials 2000

	SIT billion	%
Natural stone	0.6	9.0
Roofing tiles, bricks and other ceramic construction materials	1.2	17.9
Cement and lime manufactures	1.8	26.9
Manufactured concrete, cement and plaster products	2.9	43.2
Other	0.2	3.0
Total exports	6.7	100.0

Source: Construction and Building Materials Association, Slovenia

The construction and building materials industry is generally profitable. In 2000, the industry sector covering other mining and quarrying activities (C14) earned profits of SIT 357 million, compared to SIT 279 million for 1999. The manufacture of other non-metallic mineral products (DI26), which also includes the building materials industry, generated a net profit of SIT 5.1 million in 2000, compared to SIT 3.9 million in 1999.

The building industry needs to modernize its production facilities and production lines by advancing the technological process and improving the organization of manufacturing processes. There is also a need to cut costs in order to improve competitiveness. Both investment and exports are expected to benefit from EU membership.

Top companies

The following is a non-exhaustive list of leading Slovenian companies in the building materials industry, identified by product group.

Name	Activity
Salonit, Anhovo	Production of cement
ESAL, Anhovo	Manufacture of fibre cement products
Cementarna, Trbovlje	Production of cement
Kograd IGEM, Dravograd	Manufacture of concrete products
Stavbar IGM, Hoee	Manufacture of concrete products
Bramac, Skocjan	Manufacture of concrete tiles
Goriske Opekarne, Renee	Manufacture of brick products
Wieneberger Opekarna Orno	Manufacture of brick products
Tondach Opekarna Krizevei	Manufacture of brick tiles
Ljubeena	Manufacture of brick products
Marmor, Hotavlje	Machining of natural stone
Marmor, Sezuana	Machining of natural stone
IGM Zagorje	Manufacture of all kinds of lime
SCT IAK, Kresnice	Manufacture of all kinds of lime
Novolit, Nova vas	Production of insulating materials

4.5

Metal Products and Processing

Janos Orban

Production of machines in Slovenia

Production of machines and other working devices has a long tradition in Slovenia. In the former Yugoslav Republic this industrial branch was concentrated in some big enterprises and concerns such as Metalna, Litostroj, Tam, and Vozila Gorica.

In the time of transition there were many enterprises that failed to adapt to a new system, some stopped any business activity and some were transformed. The number of employees was actually reduced by half in that period. Those who lost their jobs were responsible for establishing many small and medium-sized enterprises which have been shown to be more flexible and can easily adapt to new market changes. Despite this, the new enterprises took over the technology and production programmes from the old enterprises, which suffered greatly for several reasons. There was a lack of funds for development and traditional markets were lost. For these reasons many enterprises have become 'Lohn' businesses, which, unfortunately, were never meant to be long-term solutions because the outputs were products with low added value. In recent years many projects have taken place in Slovenia (projects for achieving higher competition, gaining the ISO certificate...), some within the sphere of PHARE projects, Chambers of Commerce and some of the Ministries in Slovenia.

Regardless of the recession in the whole industry, the trends towards technological development in Slovenia are improving. Many enterprises are improving old programmes, implementing new ones and investing more frequently in new technology. Better business results are also achieved by employing information technology in the development phase (CAD systems) as well as in the production phase (CNC machines, flexible automation, CAD-CAM systems).

The best results have been achieved in toolmaking and the timber industry, but the rising trend can also be noticed in other sectors, in enterprises aware that there is no success without investing in knowledge and equipment. Small enterprises have also been very successful by offering not just products but also technical solutions for production automation.

A positive influence is also coming from better economic operations from some bigger systems which have connected with strategic partners (for example, Revoz with Renault, Tomos with Cimos, Gorenje with Siemens). A good sign is that they tend to use not only material but also some high-quality semi-manufacturers in Slovenia.

Table 4.5.1 Industrial production volume indices (average of previous year = 100)

	Mfr. of machinery and equipment nec.
1995	103.1
1997	88.5
1998	108.8
1999	99.4
2000	105.4
2001	115.4

Table 4.5.2 Indices of the number of persons (average of previous year = 100)

	Mfr. of machinery and equipment nec.
1997	121.7
1998	101.4
1999	99.0
2000	100.2
2001	101.9

4.6

Electronics and Electrical Engineering

TIPO

The role of electronics and electrical engineering in the economy

The Slovenian electronics and electrical engineering industry is the economy's leading export sector. More than 70 per cent of its exports are sold in the highly competitive EU and CEFTA markets. The sector generated a turnover of EUR 2.8 billion in 2001, which represented 16.3 per cent of total Slovene manufacturing industry turnover and was an increase of 22 per cent on the previous year. Over the same period the increase in gross added value per employee was 2.8 per cent.

The industry's income from export sales in 2000 totalled EUR 1.59 billion and amounted to 20.2 per cent of the total income generated by the export of manufactured products from Slovenia. The main trading partners are Germany, Italy, Austria, France and Croatia. The higher-profile export products of the Slovene electronics and electrical engineering industry and their leading manufacturers include:

- kitchen appliances: Gorenje-GA, BSH Hisni aparati;

- telecommunication exchanges: Iskratel;

- electric motors: Rotomatika, Kolektor, Iskra-Avtoelektrika, Domel;

- electrical power meters: Iskraemeco;

- capacitors: Iskra-Kondenzatorji;

- laser technology products: Fotona;

- overhead projectors and slide projectors: Vega;

- switches, heating equipment for household appliances: Metalflex, ETA;

- fuses and safety switches: ETI-Elektorelement;

- compressors for refrigeration systems: Danfoss-Compressors.

The impact of EU membership

The electronics and electrical engineering industry operates to a large extent in compliance with ISO 9000 quality assurance standards and in conformity with EU regulations. As a major exporter, this industry sector must meet the requirements of the EU single market, which entails that all EU directives must be respected. Thus, Slovenia's export-oriented companies are fully competitive in the demanding EU markets.

The sub-sector of radio stations and terminal equipment is governed by special regulations arising from the Law on Telecommunications, in respect of radio frequency licences, technical requirements for radio stations and terminal equipment.

The testing and certification of electronics and electrical products is performed by accredited laboratories.

Organization of the industry

In compliance with the law on the Chamber of Commerce and Industry of Slovenia, all economic operators whose main activity is manufacturing in the field of electronics and electrical engineering as well as optical equipment are automatically members of the Electronic and Electrical Engineering Association. Business operators whose secondary activity is the production of electrical devices and are related to the sector may also become members. Research, development and educational institutions are also involved in the work of the Association.

The products manufactured by members of the Association include the following groups or sub-groups from the Slovene Standard Classification of Activities (NACE rev.1):

- electric domestic appliances;

- office machinery;

- computers and other information-processing equipment;

- electric motors, generators and transformers;

- electricity distribution and control apparatus;

- insulated wires and cables;

- accumulators, primary cells and primary batteries;

- lighting equipment and electric lamps;

- electrical equipment for engines and vehicles;
- other electrical equipment;
- electronic valves, tubes and other electronic components;
- TV and radio transmitters, apparatus for line telephony;
- TV and radio receivers, sound and video recording apparatus;
- medical and surgical equipment and orthopaedic appliances;
- instruments and appliances for measuring, navigating, etc;
- industrial process control equipment;
- optical instruments and photographic equipment.

The employment profile of manufacturing companies in the electronics and electrical engineering industry is shown in Table 4.6.1.

Table 4.6.1 Number and employment structure of companies in the electronics and electrical engineering industry

Companies	Number of companies	Number of employees
Large	66	28,108
Medium-size	95	5,035
Small	615	2,633
Industry total	776	35,776

Source: Electronics and Electrical Engineering Association of Slovenia

Ranked according to sales turnover in 2000, the following are the top fifteen companies of the electronics and electrical engineering sector:

1. Gorenje-GA, d.d., Velenje – Household appliances
2. Iskratel, d.o.o., Kranj – Telecommunications exchanges and systems
3. Danfoss-Compressors, Ernomelj – Compressors for refrigeration systems
4. Iskraemeco, Kranj – Electric power meters
5. Iskra-Avtoelektrika, Sempeter pri Gorici – Ignitions, electric motors, alternators
6. Kolektor, Idrija – Commutators for electric motors
7. ETA, Cerkno – Thermal equipment for kitchen household appliances
8. Elektronika, Valenje – TV sets

9. Rotomatika, Spodnja Idrija – Electric motors, suction units

10. BSH Hisni Aparati, Nazarje – Small household appliances

11. Domel – Electric motors

12. ETI-Elektroelement, Izlake – Fuses, circuit breakers, safety switches

13. Saturnus-Avtooprema, Ljubljana – Lighting fixtures

14. LIV Postojna – Vacuum cleaners

15. Iskra-Kondenzatorji, Semie – Foil capacitors, RFI filters

4.7

Chemical and Rubber Industry

TIPO

Manufactured products

The chemical and rubber industry covers a highly diverse range of activities of which the manufacture of chemical products (section DG) is the most important and accounted for 64 per cent of all revenues in 2000 in the Slovenian chemical industry. In the same year, the manufacture of rubber and plastic products (section DH) accounted for the balance of 36 per cent of revenues.

In terms of production volume and business performance, the pharmaceutical industry rates highest within the sector, employing 23.6 per cent of all workers and generating 27 per cent of revenues. Pharmaceuticals also accounts for 31.6 per cent of sector exports and 41.6 per cent of profits in the overall chemical and rubber industry.

The various sub-sectors of the chemical and rubber industry are ranked in order of year 2000 revenues in Table 4.7.1.

Table 4.7.1 Types of chemical and rubber products

Manufacturing product group	Revenues in 2000 (SIT million)	Rank
Pharmaceuticals	138,592	1
Plastic products	101,139	2
Rubber products	83,720	3
Basic chemicals	63,243	4
Paints, varnishes and coatings	36,990	5
Other chemical products	33,348	6
Soap, cleaning, polishing, perfumes and toilet preparations	28,304	7
Man-made fibres	22,117	8
Pesticides and other agrochemical	6,343	9
Total revenues	513,796	–

In the same year, the chemical and rubber industry accounted for 15.5 per cent of the revenues generated by all Slovenian manufacturing industries and for 5.3 per cent of total revenues of industry and commerce.

Foreign trade

The chemical and rubber industrial sector is strongly export-oriented with exports of USD 1,420 million in 2000 far exceeding USD 886 million worth of goods imported into Slovenia. However, the total import of chemical products in 2000, including finished goods, was USD 1,392 million.

The leading export products by volume are pharmaceuticals and semi-products used in the manufacture of pharmaceuticals, car tyres, basic chemicals, plastic products, chemical fibres, paints and varnishes, other chemical products, detergents and cosmetics. The main imports are raw materials, such as sulphur, boron and titanium ores, aluminium oxide and hydroxide, sodium hydroxide, orthoxylene, caprolactam and other petrochemicals, basic polymers (plastics) and pharmaceutical substances, as well as many chemical semi-finished and finished products.

The industry's main trading partners by volume of trade in 2000 were Germany, Croatia, Italy, Poland, the Russian Federation, Austria, Bosnia and Herzegovina, the Czech Republic, Hungary, Macedonia and France.

Chemical and rubber industry manufacturers

The Chemical and Rubber Industry Association numbers among its membership around 120 manufacturing companies and 480 small producers of chemical and other related products. Together, these companies employ a workforce of 21,390 and generated net profits of SIT 26,606 million in 2000 on revenues of SIT 513,796 million.

In Table 4.7.2, the financial profile of the industry is displayed. The data are drawn from the closing profit and loss accounts of Chemical and Rubber Industry Association members.

Table 4.7.2 Financial profile of chemical and rubber manufacturers, 2000

	Value SIT million	Share in all manufacturing industry %
Total revenues	513,796	15.5
Revenues on foreign markets	309,669	18.0
Net profit	32,417	26.1
Net loss	5,536	10.8
Added value	156,182	17.5
(No. employees)	(23,178)	11.0
Added value/employee	6,738	–

4.8

Pulp, Paper and Paper Converting

TIPO

The industry

Slovenia has a four-century tradition in its pulp, paper and paper-converting industry. Its progressive development is founded on the available raw materials, power supply, the development of chemical and other related industries, suitable infrastructure and a highly skilled workforce. A reputation for good product quality is a guarantee for the success of this branch of industry on both the home Slovene and foreign markets, in particular in Europe.

The seven pulp and paper factories in Slovenia have capacities as follows:

- paper and cardboard 600,000 tons/year, of which:

  - newsprint: 14 per cent;

  - writing/printing paper: 46 per cent;

  - personal hygiene paper: 13 per cent;

  - packaging paper: 2 per cent;

  - cardboard and pasteboard: 25 per cent;

- paper and lumber 170,000 tons/year, of which:

  - pulp: 82 per cent;

  - lumber: 18 per cent.

The paper- and cardboard-converting industry segment numbers 22 large and about 40 small companies with the following total combined capacities:

- corrugated cardboard: 75,000 tons;

- corrugated cardboard products: 80,000 tons;

- other paper, cardboard in pasteboard products: 100,000 tons.

This segment employs 6,000 persons and its share of the net revenue of Slovene processing industries is 4 per cent. Approximately 63 per cent of its sales are exported.

Paper and paper-converting industry product lines

The total diverse range of paper and converted paper product lines produced in Slovenia includes all of the following:

- bleached and non-bleached sulphite pulp, lumber;

- one- and two-side coated paper, wood-free and printing paper, continuous paper, copying paper, newsprint paper, recycled paper, basic self-copying paper for CB and CF, stock and safety paper, wrapping paper, personal hygiene paper;

- grey and white pasteboard, surface-coloured in enamelled pasteboard;

- coated cardboard for folding boxes, grey cardboard, cardboard;

- two-, three-, five-layer corrugated cardboard with B, C and E cylinders;

- self-adhesive paper, foil, labels, personal hygiene paper products, envelopes, notepads, wrapping paper, plastic cards, pasteboard products, paper stationery, folders, rolls, bags, cardboard tubes, wallpaper, self-copy paper;

- toilet paper, handkerchiefs, napkins and other personal hygiene paper products;

- corrugated cardboard packaging, printed and non-printed packaging, merchandise cardboard packaging, transport packaging, pasteboard, packaging for liquid products, line paper packaging, paper packaging, spiral tubes.

International trade

In 2001, Slovenia's pulp, paper and paper-converting industry was a net exporter, with exports of EUR 400,000 offset by imports with a value of EUR 300,000. The top eight export markets and import sources are detailed in Table 4.8.1.

Table 4.8.1 Leading foreign trade partners in pulp and converted paper products

	Import sources %	Export markets %
Germany	17	12
Croatia	6	18
Italy	17	13
FR Yugoslavia	–	6
Bosnia and Herzegovina	–	6
Hungary	–	5
UK	–	5
Austria	14	4
Czech Republic	7	–
Poland	5	–
Finland	4	–
Netherlands	4	–
Other countries	26	31

4.9

Insurance

TIPO

A short history of the insurance sector

The hundredth anniversary of the first completely Slovenian insurance company was celebrated in 2000. As an economic sector the insurance business has an even longer tradition on Slovenian soil, with approximately 25 foreign insurance companies or their subsidiaries in operation at the end of the 19th century. The number dwindled after World War I and after World War II the newly formed Yugoslav socialist state was abandoned by foreign insurance companies. Indigenous Slovenian insurance companies functioned as a part of the State Insurance Institute headquartered in Belgrade.

The insurance sector experienced a number of legal changes during the socialist period which affected its organization but had a lesser influence on its business activity, which was based on reciprocity. More revolutionary changes took place in the industry after the retreat of communism at the end of the 1980s and the first joint-stock insurance companies reappeared towards the end of 1990. Some of these companies were established by Slovene owners. Others were set up with majority Slovenian capital and minority foreign investment; still others were formed with majority foreign capital. This diversity remains today.

One effect of the emergence of independent Slovenia was that the insurance guarantee of the Yugoslav Federal Insurance Bureau ceased, so that it became imperative for Slovenia to establish its own Green Card Bureau. Members of this bureau, formed in 1992, were insurance companies engaged in performing motor third-party liability insurance. The Bureau soon evolved into an association representing the interests of all active insurance companies and is now called the Slovenian Insurance Association, GIZ (economic interest association), within which the Green Card Bureau is an organizational unit that performs the tasks specified in the adopted international agreements regulating the insurance of motor vehicles against liability for third-party damages.

Legislation

In the decade since 1992 the Slovenian insurance business has been regulated by two state system Acts which took effect in 1994 and 2000. The old Yugoslav legislation remained in force until the enactment of the first law. The current Insurance Act now in force (*Official Gazette of the Republic of Slovenia*, no. 13/2000 and 20 regulatory decrees) conforms almost entirely to the EU legislation.

Together with some other Acts which affect the development and organization of insurance business, the new regulation has brought about great changes in the business operations of Slovenian insurance companies, of which the main characteristics are:

• the complete opening of the Slovenian insurance market in the face of European competition and the harmonization of the Slovenian insurance sector with EU directives and legislation;

• new opportunities for an even more successful development of the life insurance sector (above all pension insurance) by means of incentive tax legislation;

• the withdrawal of state control over the motor third-party liability insurance premiums;

• a new supervisory system, undertaken by the Agency for Insurance Business Supervision.

In spite of the many legislative changes, the business activities of insurance and re-insurance companies pursued their profitable way through the turn of the millennium with the increased growth of gross premiums from written insurance and re-insurance business, technical provisions, capital enhancement and net insurance and re-insurance profits which totalled SIT 5.3 billion. The year 2000 also marked the beginning of the process of merger or concentration of insurance companies, with the new Act enabling the biggest companies to expand in foreign markets.

Structure of the insurance industry

By July 2001 there were 17 insurance and re-insurance companies operating in Slovenia, but in 2002 the number had reduced to 13. Of those remaining, 11 were commercial or other insurance companies and members of the Slovenian Insurance Association, and 2 were re-insurance companies.

Insurance companies market 24 kinds of insurance under the new Insurance Act, divided into the two main groups of life and non-life insurance. The majority of the insurance companies belong to the non-life group, which generates 80 per cent of total gross premiums, although their share in the premiums of the aggregate portfolio has decreased steadily as the share of the life assurance group has increased. Of the composite or general non-life insurance companies, one is specialized in health insurance only and one (Slovene Export Corporation) in the insurance of export business against commercial and non-commercial risks.

After authorized investment companies, insurance and re-insurance companies form the second largest group of non-banking financial brokers. Insurance business units are concentrated in the larger town residential areas and their services are offered in some five hundred locations. There is a concentration of almost 2.5 per cent business units per 100 square kilometres. Distribution of the aggregate insurance portfolio is asymmetric, with the largest insurance company's market share in 2002 being 43 per cent in terms of aggregate gross premiums and the combined market share of the three largest insurance companies amounting to 78 per cent. The total share of the eight remaining insurance companies is therefore only 22 per cent.

The three principal non-life insurance companies, in terms of year 2000 market share, are Triglav (40.3 per cent), Health Insurance Mutual (26.8 per cent) and Maribor (11.3 per cent). Insurance companies with majority foreign capital, such as Generali, Merkur and Grawe, are important but their market share remains relatively small.

The proportion of foreign investment in the capital of Slovenian insurance companies at 27 per cent is now comparable to foreign insurance investment in the majority of EU member states.

Statistics

The gross premiums written by all insurance companies in 2000 in Slovenia from about 3 million contracts amounted to more than SIT 192 billion (non-life SIT 155 billion; life SIT 37 billion). This outcome represents a 12.5 per cent increase over 1999 and is nearly 17 times the comparable figure from 1991. Premium growth in 2000 was 3.6 per cent higher than inflation and nearly 10 per cent was generated by the re-insurance market. Although still above the inflation rate, non-life insurance premiums increased by a lesser 10.7 per cent in 2000.

The share of the insurance sector in Slovenia's GDP increased to 4.77 per cent in 2000. Numerous cases of damage caused the amount of gross claims to rise sharply by 21 per cent, from SIT 104 billion to SIT 126 billion. Subsequently, the ratio of claims to premiums depreciated from 61 to 65 per cent.

In terms of collected premiums, the voluntary health insurance group is ranked first among all insurance groups, with 2000 premiums of almost SIT 50 billion, representing a 25.9 per cent market share. Life insurance held second place with premiums of SIT 37.2 billion (19.4

per cent), while motor insurance premiums at SIT 34 billion (17.7 per cent) ranked third.

Together with voluntary health insurance and accident insurance, life insurance has become an increasingly important element of personal insurance. With combined 2000 premiums at SIT 101.9 billion, they already account for a 52.8 per cent share in the aggregate portfolio.

4.10

Transport and Communications

TIPO

Slovenia's strategic location at the very intersection of international commercial currents in Europe affords great potential with its ready access to a land area of 19.5 million km² and a market of more than 400 million inhabitants. The countries which are already, or will become in less than a year, members of the EU and its wider-world economic integration together import and export more than USD 1,030 billion worth of goods each year. Although levels of growth among most existing EU members are currently depressed, standards of living remain high and are growing among the new entrants. Slovenia also benefits from a rich background of excellent logistical and telecommunication connections, which have helped to secure its position as the most prosperous of the CEE states that are scheduled for EU membership in 2004.

Goods, money, expertise, experience and information are all exchanged in this area of Central Europe where business connections between partners from Central and Eastern Europe and the rest of the commercial world are forged. Slovenia represents an attractive business crossroads where its logistical capabilities, available 24 hours a day, 365 days a year, prepare goods for direct selling and perform added-value services which extend from the fast transmission of goods to the customer to marketing, commercial, financial, investment and information support. Employees of Slovenian logistical operators are conscious that qualitative excellence in the performance of their work is the key to customer satisfaction and provide services to international standards.

An overview of service offers in Slovenia

The following registered business services are provided by companies active within the Transport and Communications Association:

Railway transportation: contractors organize freight transportation by rail to all European countries, part of Asia and the Middle East by freight wagons and containers. 'Direct complete trains' are offered for freight transportation from Western European countries through Slovenia.

Sea and coastal water transportation: freight services (general, bulk cargo and permanent import, export and transit loads) are offered by sea and coastal water.

Air transport: It is possible to hire part-charter or full-charter plane space and, in addition, regular import and export lines of air collection, freight and passenger transportation services to a guaranteed 100 countries. A wide and diverse network of international connections with air carriers and airports worldwide enables a constant supervision of consignments to be carried out. Upon reaching the country, an express delivery service which consigns goods to any world destination ensures that the consignment does not remain stuck in the warehouse.

Freight and passenger transportation by road: contractors organize urban and suburban scheduled and special transportation services with modern buses and coaches across Slovenia and European countries. Freight transportation services are also available across Slovenia, European countries, the other countries of the former Yugoslavia, the Middle East and the Commonwealth of Independent States (comprising Russia and 11 former Soviet republics). Vehicles are equipped for the transportation of dangerous substances in compliance with the ARD convention and are additionally equipped with the latest telecommunications technology (GPS, GSM, SMS), which allows the monitoring of the location and status of freight at any instant.

Cargo handling: contractors of cargo handling services are qualified to handle general cargoes, cars, fruit and perishables, cattle, various ores, cereals, and liquid cargoes.

Storage and warehousing: in numerous storage facilities across the country, the storage of goods is performed in covered and uncovered warehouses, silos and reservoirs, where goods are repacked and, if required, their manufacture completed.

Post and courier services: postal and courier services related to letters and parcels weighing up to 32 kilograms are carried out by door-to-door delivery. These services are supported by a network of distribution centres, connected by an information centre, which enables the monitoring of consignments at any moment.

Forwarding agency activities: contractors of forwarding agency services traditionally perform tasks involving the organization of transport and customs agents' services in all the regular kinds of import and export of goods and in procedures with economic outcomes.

Skilled, trained staff provide the additional information required for the speedy realization of customs procedures, counselling services for the application of customs regulations, customs tariffing of goods and preparation of certificates of origin.

Some contractors also operate as authorized forwarding agents according to simplified customs procedures such as authorized senders and recipients, which permit a simplified transit procedure and declaration of goods to be carried out, based on bookkeeping entries denoting temporary storage or the procedure of customs warehousing. The organization and realization of entire logistical projects involves all phases of circulation of goods between the producer and the customer.

Performance of the industry

In 2000, there were 1,949 companies in Slovenia's transport industry, of which 46 were classified as large, 114 medium-sized and 1,789 small. Together they accounted for 5.17 per cent of all commercial companies registered in Slovenia.

At the end of 2000, there were 37,986 workers employed in all transport activities, representing 8.11 per cent of the employed national workforce. The industry's assets were valued at SIT 1,051 billion at that date, representing 9.7 per cent of the economy's entire asset base. Capital assets (12.37 per cent of the national total) were valued at SIT 857 billion. After-tax profits of the transport industry reached SIT 29 billion in 2000, accounting for 9.55 per cent of the economy's total profit. Non-operating losses were SIT 13 billion (7.04 per cent of the economy's), and value added amounted to SIT 209 billion, which was 10.2 per cent of the economy's entire value added.

4.11

Real Estate

TIPO

As in all developed economies, real estate business in Slovenia comprises activities such as buying, selling, leasing, exchanging and letting of land and developed industrial, commercial and residential property. Real estate management services include negotiation and mediation in transactions, valuations, investment structuring and related maintenance.

Services

Business transactions involving own real estate

The range of own account transactions consists of:

- organization of commercial property development schemes (services involving the promotion of property investment projects);

- coordination (network management) of financial, technical and physical resources for the implementation of commercial property development schemes;

- buying and selling of own real estate (treated as selling stock and not as disposals of fixed assets):
  - residential blocks and detached houses complete with surrounding plots;
  - non-residential buildings complete with plots comprising factories, warehouses, multipurpose buildings, offices, agricultural and forest land, and similar estates;
  - individual apartments or apartment block floors;
  - plots for housing purposes and other undeveloped sites;

- renting own real estate or letting on lease and real estate management:
  - residential blocks and apartments;

- non-residential buildings, including exhibition and trade halls;

- trade and exhibition grounds;

- land or plots for development;

- time-sharing lease activities, including halls of residence for students, old people and single people's homes and residential hotels;

- rented space for residential trailers, garages and parking lots.

Third-party business transactions against payment or under contract

Real estate agency activities:

● intermediary in buying, selling and leasing of real estate (buildings, land or plots);

● trading of undeveloped sites;

● valuation of real estate (buildings and undeveloped sites).

Real estate management against payment or under contract:

● management of residential real estate;

● management of business buildings and industrial facilities, multi-purpose buildings, including agricultural and forest land and similar real estate;

● rent collection.

Foreigners' rights in the Slovenian real estate market

The current regulatory system in the Republic of Slovenia is among those that, as a rule, do not allow foreigners to acquire proprietorship rights in real estate. However, there has been gradual progress towards liberalization and entry to the EU in May 2004 will signal equal rights for all EU citizens. Until then, regulations at present in force permit real estate in Slovenia to be acquired by:

● EU citizens, subject to the proviso that they may only purchase real estate under conditions of reciprocity and that applicants have resided in Slovenia for a minimum of three years;

● citizens of all countries entitled to succession;

● foreign countries for the purpose of performing their diplomatic and consular activities.

There are special stipulations in the Association Agreement between Slovenia and EU member states that make it impossible, until 1 January 2005, for citizens and enterprises with their headquarters in the EU to set up real estate businesses in Slovenia. Otherwise, there are no legal impediments to foreign direct investment into real estate that are required for the performance of all activities of corporations established by foreigners in compliance with Slovenia's Companies Act.

The housing market

Following the completion of extensive mass privatization in the early 1990s, over 80 per cent of Slovenian inhabitants have been residing in their own flats. Even in the 1980s, before the privatization process was carried out, private ownership had reached 67 per cent, a level comparable with most Western European countries. However, the Slovenian housing market is still unbalanced. With its social policies and a partly state-owned banking industry, the general demand for housing loans is constantly increasing, while the supply of housing remains inadequately financed.

Under the National Housing Programme, approved by the Slovenian Parliament, a target of 10,000 new residential flats per annum was set. However, up to 2002, Slovenia had not yet managed to build as many as 4,000 flats in any year since the introduction of the market economy.

The rise of the private house leasing sector is important for the further balancing of housing market development. It would reduce significantly the rate of demand for own flats and thereby cause market prices to fall. Development of this sector also provides an excellent foreign investment opportunity for banks, insurance companies, investment companies and funds, construction companies and the building materials industry. Already, the increased demand for housing, together with a greater involvement of Slovenian civil engineering abroad, has fuelled an increase of 3.5 per cent in the construction and building materials industry, with further growth of 4 per cent forecast for 2003.

4.12

Tourism

TIPO

The year 2000 was the most successful year for Slovenian tourism since independence was gained in 1991. The number of foreign visitors was higher than in 1997, the previous most successful year since independence, and marked a recovery from 1999 and 1998, which were affected by the negative influence of war in Yugoslavia. As Table 4.12.1 demonstrates, the number of overnight stays in 2000 rose by 5 per cent compared to 1997, with an 11 per cent increase in the number of foreign guests and only a minimal increase in the number of domestic guests. Historically, 1986 was the best tourist year ever for Slovenia when it was still a part of Yugoslavia.

Table 4.12.1 Tourists and their overnight stays in Slovenia in selected years

	('000)				
	1986	1990	1997	1999	2000
Tourists					
Foreign	2,038	1,885	974	884	1,098
Domestic	783	651	849	865	877
All	2,821	2,536	1,823	1,749	1,975
Overnight stays					
Foreign	6,277	5,345	3,078	2,741	3,404
Domestic	2,936	2,611	3,306	3,315	3,315
All	9,213	7,956	6,384	6,056	6,719

Visitors and overnight stays

Strategically, the most significant development was the comparatively high increase in the number of visitors from all neighbouring countries. Both Italian and Hungarian visitors increased in number by 21 per cent, comparing 2000 with 1997, while the number of visitors from Croatia and Austria increased by 18 and 9 per cent respectively. The economic significance of the Slovenian tourist offering has therefore gained in importance.

Indeed, the ratio between foreign and domestic tourism changed in 2000 to the advantage of foreign tourism, being 56:44 with regard to the number of tourists and 51:49 with regard to overnight stays. The average period of guest stays in 2000 was closely similar to 1999 at 3.4 days. On average, domestic guests occupied tourist facilities for 3.8 days, compared with 3.1 days by foreign visitors.

The most important Slovenian tourist resorts reflect the positive trend in the number of visitors. In 2000, 27 resorts reported more than 50,000 overnight stays, of which 15 resorts recorded 100,000 or more. Among the 15 are the capital Ljubljana, five spas (Catez, Moravske Toplice, Terme Olimia, Rogaska Slatina and Radenci), four seaside resorts (Portoroz, Izola, Ankaran and Strunjan) and three mountain resorts (Bled, Kranjska Goa and Bohini).

The Upper Carniola locations are the most orientated towards attracting foreign visitors, so it is not surprising that they were the most affected by political crisis in 1999, before recovering in 2000. In 2000, overnight stays in Kranjska Gora increased by 6 per cent compared with 1997, with a 20 per cent increase in foreign visitor overnight stays. Bled and Bohinj also benefited from a good summer season in 2000 compared with 1997, with increases of 9 and 3 per cent respectively in overnight stays by foreign guests.

Hotel tourism

The most important sector in the national tourist economy, in terms of commercial income, is hotel tourism. In 2000 there were 13,462 hotel rooms, which represented 45 per cent of all rooms available to tourists. The total number of permanent beds was 24,361, which accounted for one-third of all tourist beds. Hotels reported 4,222,248 overnight stays in 2000, which represented 63 per cent of all overnight stays (being 74 per cent of all foreign and 51 per cent of all domestic overnight stays). Over three years the number of total overnight stays in Slovenian hotels had increased by 7 per cent, with domestic overnight stays rising by 4 per cent and foreign overnight stays by 9 per cent.

Foreign exchange inflows

The most important indicators of the benefits that tourism brings to the economy are the statistics for foreign exchange inflows, which are detailed in Table 4.12.2.

Table 4.12.2 Tourist foreign exchange inflows in 2000

	US$000	Index 2000/1999	%
Tourist companies	108,698	114	11
Duty-free sales	79,716	86	8
Gaming houses	131,645	82	14
Health services	10,196	201	1
Educational services	4,202	143	0
Other credit card debits	63,006	170	7
Cash in tolars	425,299	102	45
Other	134,068	95	14
Total inflow	956,830	100	100

The foreign exchange expenditure of Slovenian citizens abroad must be accounted for against revenues from foreign tourists. In 2000 the outflow of tourist foreign exchange is estimated to have been USD 517,243, representing 54 per cent of the total foreign exchange inflow but a decline of 4 per cent on 1999.

4.13

Management Consultancy

Association of Management Consulting of Slovenia (AMCOS)

The management consulting environment

In May 2003, the management consulting industry in Slovenia achieved prominence when the Association of Management Consulting of Slovenia (AMCOS) organized and hosted the annual conference of the European Federation of Management Consultancy Associations (FEACO) in Ljubljana on the occasion of the tenth anniversary of its FEACO membership.

Management consulting in Slovenia is still in a growth phase, unlike some West European countries where the sector still suffers the after-shock of the crisis which afflicted the industry in North America in 2001/2 in the form of the fraudulent accounting scandals within US multinationals which brought down the venerable Arthur Andersen accountancy firm. The subsequent fall-out for major global consulting practices is still reverberating and has generated a closer scrutiny of best practice and international standards within both the consulting and accountancy industries.

The membership of AMCOS doubled over four years to 66 firms, employing more than 600, at the beginning of 2003, while business increased at a rate of nearly 30 per cent in 2001, although growth fell back to 13 per cent in 2002. Looking ahead to the next few years, AMCOS anticipates an increased demand for consulting, mainly in the public sector, with a focus on finance and taxes, strategic planning, marketing and sales in the context of alignment with the EU and the extension of operations. As in other European markets, the most successful consulting firms are manifestly those which offer fast, quality and integral solutions, especially in the field of reorganization, the rationalization of operations, the introduction of quality systems and customer strategies.

The main drivers for further growth of the consulting sector throughout Europe are perceived by FEACO to be:

- introduction of the single European currency;

- dynamic development of the Eastern European economies;

- continuing enlargement of the EU to Central, Eastern and South-Eastern Europe;

- continued globalization.

With the Swedish referendum vote against joining the eurozone and less urgency on the part of the EU new entrants to adopt the euro, the first of these drivers seems to have weakened for the time being. The failure of the WTO meeting in Cancun in September 2003 has also cast a shadow over the prospects for removal of barriers to international trade in the foreseeable future.

Consulting activity in Slovenia

Management consulting is among Slovenia's most dynamic economic activities. The average growth rate in the five years up to 2003 was 15 per cent, with the highest rate of 29 per cent in 2001. Even in the general economic slowdown of 2002 AMCOS members' 15 per cent growth in activity generated EUR 55 million of total income, representing about 0.24 per cent of GDP. A similar outcome for 2003 is expected.

Although Slovenian management consulting companies operate mainly in the domestic market, some 7 per cent of total income was generated outside Slovenia in 2002 in the EU, EFTA and SEE countries. In Slovenia, as elsewhere, the market is becoming increasingly demanding. Clients seek more and more adapted services, and confidence and service quality are paramount. There is a growing tendency to structure projects on a shared-risk basis with consultants. Short-term small-scale projects have also been a feature of the uncertain business environment since 2001. Many large projects have been postponed or restructured into smaller projects.

Demand has increased mostly in operations management and the fields of mergers and acquisitions, market communications and research, human relations management (HRM), business process re-engineering, legal consulting and financial advisory work. EU accession will be an important push factor on the demand side, with more projects in business re-engineering, market research and product development. Among the most important industry sectors for management consulting client development will be energy, pharmaceuticals, the media, services in general, entertainment and tourism. Institutional clients are expected to continue playing an important role as well.

Table 4.13.1 provides a breakdown of the income of AMCOS members in 2002 into the basic fields of consulting.

Table 4.13.1 AMCOS 2002 income by consulting field

	%
Corporate strategy services	59
Operations management	28
Human resources	8
Information technology	4
Outsourcing services	1
	100

The dominant field of corporate strategy services is broken down further in Table 4.13.2.

Table 4.13.2 Composition of corporate strategy consulting income 2002

	%
Strategic planning/organizational development	40
Mergers and acquisitions	14
Financial advisory services	12
Sales/marketing/corporate communication	10
Market and competitive intelligence	10
Other (eg market research)	14
	100

Similarly, the second most pervasive field of consulting income, operations management, is broken down in Table 4.13.3.

Table 4.13.3 Composition of operations management consulting income 2000

	%
Business process re-engineering	51
Change management	14
Project management	14
Purchasing and supply management	7
Turnaround/cost reduction	7
Customer/supplier relationship management	7
	100

Advantages for clients in working with AMCOS members

Consulting companies which are AMCOS members are recognized on the basis of the quality of consulting assignments they perform and references given by clients. They are experts in different specialized fields. In the local context, they are the most knowledgeable assessors of the economic situation, structure and trends and of business practices through their wide network of local and regional business relationships. Internationally, many of them participate in consultancy projects on a permanent basis.

Consultants are qualified according to European standards and perform consulting assignments to an international code of practice. Approximate average fees for the consulting services of AMCOS members in 2002 are summarized in Table 4.13.4.

Table 4.13.4 Consulting fees of AMCOS members 2002 (excluding VAT, travel expenses, daily allowances and material costs)

	Small and medium MC firms EUR per day	Top MC firms/complex project EUR per day
Junior consultant	230	400
Consultant	350	600
Project manager	550	900
Partner consultant	750	1,200

4.14

Trade Exhibitions in Slovenia

Robert Otorepec, Celski Sejem d.d.

A short history of fairs and exhibitions in Slovenia

The tradition of trade fairs in the territory of present-day Slovenia goes far back to the Middle Ages, all the way to the 10th century, when Radgona was granted the right to hold an annual fair. During most of the Middle Ages, Slovenia was part of the Austrian Empire and, like other towns in the Austrian Empire, Slovenian towns and marketplaces were granted rights by the rulers to hold annual fairs.

In the 15th century, Celje was granted the right to hold seven annual fairs. Until that time, no other Slovenian town had held so many fairs. In Ljubljana, for example, five annual fairs were held in the 16th century. Kranj, which was granted the right to hold two fairs yearly, retained the trade fair tradition throughout the centuries and even expanded in the 17th and 18th centuries to become the leading Slovenian town of trade fairs for agricultural crops, especially for wheat and livestock. More important fairs in the Middle Ages were also held in Maribor and Slovenj Gradec. These were fairs of the medieval type, the basic purpose of which was the promotion of trade and the exchange of commodities.

The first modern-type fairs began to appear in the territory of Slovenia at the beginning of the 19th century. In Ljubljana, fairs for Illyric wines enjoyed great popularity. In Gornja Radgona, a large agricultural exhibition coupled with the assessment of agricultural crops and livestock was organized as early as 1876, and major horse races were held there as well. In Celje, the first modern-type fair event was organized in 1863.

With the entry of Slovenia into the Kingdom of Serbs, Croats and Slovenes in 1918, trade fair organizing companies, which still operate today, started to be established in the larger towns of the newly created state. The Ljubljana Fair was established in 1921, and as early as 1925 it became the founding member of the UFI (Union des Foires Internationales), the most important international trade fair association. In 1922, the Zagreb Fair was founded, and the Novi Sad and the Belgrade fairs soon followed suit. Up to the Second World War, the larger international trade fairs in the territory of Slovenia were held only in Ljubljana. After the Second World War, however, new trade fair centres appeared in Slovenia once again. In 1951, the Gorenjsko Fair was created. The organizing of trade fairs was started in Maribor in 1955, and in Celje in 1968.

During the period of Socialist Yugoslavia from 1945 to 1991, fairs experienced a rapid growth, since they represented one of the few promotional channels available at the time. In the then Yugoslavia, large shopping centres and modern marketing methods did not yet exist and the demand for modern goods exceeded their supply. The rapid development of fairs during that period was characteristic not only of Slovenia and the former Yugoslavia but also of the whole world.

With the emergence of the independent Slovenian state in 1991, new development opportunities also opened up in the area of trade fairs. A boom followed, which in the years 1991–96 strengthened the position of some existing fairs and also ushered in numerous new trade fair programmes. With the emergence of independent Slovenia, the imports regime was liberalized and fairs became a place where all kinds of merchandise from all over the world were available. Fairs became a mass meeting place for visitors, since they represented an opportunity to purchase goods which in the former state had been burdened with high customs duties or had not been not available at all. Among them there were, of course, also quite a lot of cheap goods of doubtful quality and origin which offered various resellers and vendors the opportunity of making big profits.

Owing to the great demand by exhibitors for exhibition space and the large attendance, the fairs presented an excellent opportunity for organizers to make quick money, and virtually every larger place in Slovenia was soon organizing a trade fair of its own. The majority of those fairs carried out the mere function of trade. Most of them lacked the minimum infrastructure necessary for organizing fairs; nor had they any specialist staff with knowledge and experience in trade fair activity. This resulted in increasing confusion in the trade fair industry sector. All of a sudden there were over 100 fair events in Slovenia. Exhibitors and visitors were faced with the dilemma of which trade fairs they should attend, since the dates of many of them overlapped and also, in many cases, their quality was highly questionable.

Present state of Slovenian trade fair activity

The situation in the sector began to normalize in 1997, coinciding with the occurrence of recession in the global trade fair industry. In 1997, for the first time after 40 years of uninterrupted trade fair industry growth, ie growth in the number of exhibitors and the number of exhibition stands, the upward trend slowed down, while in terms of the number of visitors the figures even declined. The reason for the recession of recent years on a global scale was the development of international telecommunications, primarily the Internet and e-trade, which it seemed at first would become a substitute for fairs. Soon, however, it was found that technology could not replace the greatest advantage of fairs – personal contact. Therefore, as early as 2000, figures at the most important international trade fairs began once again to register positive growth. However, the renewed growth was not the same everywhere but in line with the economic results achieved in individual industries and countries.

The terrorist attack on the World Trade Center (WTC) in September 2001 dealt a severe blow to trade fair activity. Figures in all the key trade fair countries turned down; in Germany the number of square metres of exhibition space sold declined for the first time. The trade fair industry in the USA was hit worst by the attack on the WTC, and the downturn reflected the recession of the entire US economy. However, consequences of the recession are also being felt in Germany, which so far has no real competitors in trade fair activity.

In Slovenia, the recession in trade fair activity was due only to a small extent to the reasons that had generated the crisis in the global trade fair arena. Up to 1997, trade fairs in Slovenia had mainly carried out the function of trade rather than their basic function as an exchange of information. With the emergence of large shopping centres, Slovenian trade fairs lost their attraction for the masses, since today large shopping malls offer the wide range of goods that, until then, had been offered only by trade fairs. Moreover, shopping malls offer them every day and collect no admission or parking fees. At the same time, import and consumer protection laws became increasingly strict, which reduced the opportunities to resell commodities of doubtful quality.

The majority of fairs were not prepared for this change or were unable to adapt themselves to the new circumstances, since there were simply far too many of them in Slovenia. In 1995, there were as many as 11 trade fair organizers in Slovenia (Ljubljanski Sejem, Infos, Primorski Sejem, Gorenjski Sejem, Celjski Sejem, Cespo, STEP, Sejmar, Mariborski Sejem, Pomurski Sejem, Krebs s.p.) which organized a total of 77 fairs (not counting the regional or local trade shows) a year. Many of these fairs were without the minimum infrastructure necessary for organizing fairs.

With the Slovenian trade fairs starting to assume the basic purpose and function of trade fairs in developed countries, it meant that they ceased to generate high direct profits for trade fair owners, since contemporary trade fairs require huge investments in the infrastructure of the fairgrounds and of the local environment. It is true that fairs are primarily intended for exhibitors and visitors, but in fact they bring far greater benefits to the town, the region and the country in which they are held than to the visitors, the exhibitors and the organizer. As a result, in most countries trade fairs are regarded as enterprises of special public interest. This is why towns and regions often appear as investors and landowners. Consequently, only those fairs that were sufficiently strong financially and were also given substantial support by the local government have survived in Slovenia.

Testimony to this fact is that during the past five years Sejmar has ceased operations, Mariborski Sejem had disengaged from organizing trade fairs even before that, Celjski Sejem bought STEP in 2000 and transferred its trade fairs to Celje, since no fairground is available in Maribor at present, and in 2003 Gorenjski Sejem also ceased carrying on business. This year, Celjski Sejem also bought out the majority share in the company Cespo from the Munich-based company GHM, so that it now holds a 90 per cent share in Cespo. Primorski Sejem is becoming the organizer of a local event only and cannot be ranked among fair organizers on a national or international scale, whereas Infos will have to be moved to the location of Gospodarsko Razstavišče, since Cankarjev Dom (a cultural and convention centre) does not meet the requirements of contemporary trade fair activity. Moreover, owing to the small size of the Slovenian market, there is no room for more than 10 to 15 trade fair events of international importance in Slovenia.

At present, Slovenia has nearly completed the restructuring of its trade fair industry, which started in Western Europe 30 years ago. Fairs are gradually approaching their goal and assuming the basic role which they have everywhere in the world. This means that in order to organize trade fairs it is necessary to have a contemporary fairground, well-trained specialist staff, adequate infrastructure in the local environment and suitable trade fair programmes. In Slovenia, only three locations meet all these prerequisites at least partially – those of Celje, Ljubljana and Gornja Radgona, which were also able to adapt their fairs to contemporary expectations and requirements.

The return on the capital invested by a town or region is not measured by the direct profitability of invested capital but rather by the advantages that towns and regions derive from fairs. The real criteria are not the organizer's profit but the occupation and utilization of exhibition space, and for international fairs, their importance and benefits to the town and the region. The income of the local environment and the region from a fair exceeds by at least 10 times the income of the fair organizer.

If we take the company STEP as an example and consider that during the past few years STEP's income has amounted to over SIT 100 million, it can be deduced that through the transfer of STEP's fairs to Celje the town of Maribor has lost an income of at least SIT 1 billion a year. Therefore, further development of fairs in Slovenia largely and primarily depends on whether or not the municipal authorities in Ljubljana, Celje and Gornja Radgona will be sufficiently aware of the benefits that fairs bring to the local environment and whether or not they will be able to provide enough funds to ensure their further development. This does not only involve direct investments into the fairground's infrastructure but in the first place the improvement of the infrastructure and the provision of public services in the town as required by contemporary fairs. The organizer can only influence a part of the fair's provision of services, but the town must assume the leading role in harmonizing the entire provision of the necessary public services.

All three Slovenian towns have at their disposal approximately the same area of covered permanent exhibition space, ie 22,000 to 25,000 m^2 of gross exhibition area. Celjski Sejem and Pomurski Sejem in Gornja Radgona have an additional 25,000 m^2 approximately of outdoor exhibition areas each, which enables them to erect temporary halls to satisfy the needs of larger trade fairs. Thus, Celjski Sejem can cater for the needs of the International Trade Fair, which is the largest in Slovenia in terms of the number of exhibition stands, the number of exhibitors and the number of visitors, by providing an additional 35,000 m^2 of covered exhibition area. The Ljubljana fairground is situated in the very centre of the city, where it has at its disposal an outdoor exhibition area of only 5,000 m^2.

The most modern, well-equipped fairground in Slovenia is that of Celje, on which, in 1999, the only exhibition hall developed in Slovenia within the past 15 years was built. The hall has an area 10,000 m^2, is fully air-conditioned and is the only one in Slovenia which is comparable to more recent exhibition halls around the world.

In spite of a rapid decrease in the number of trade fairs, exhibitors and visitors, it already became clear to a great extent in 2002, and especially in 2003, which of the Slovenian fairs would survive and develop successfully. So, we can already mention some fairs which are truly international and are also suitable for participation by foreign companies wishing to enter and strengthen their position in the Slovenian market.

Such a one is the International Trade Fair in Celje, which is the largest business event in Slovenia. The fair has developed from an exhibition by small and medium-size businessmen and tradesmen to today's general fair which covers almost all areas of economy. Although general fairs are experiencing a decline in Slovenia and elsewhere, the International Trade Fair, due to its tradition, has maintained a large number of visitors and exhibitors, and is still very interesting to exhibitors from various industries. On the other hand, some major specialized fairs have already taken shape and are expanding in parallel with the development of the respective industries that they cover. Mention should be made of the Agricultural and Food Fair in Gornja Radgona, the Megra Fair (a construction and building materials fair) in Gornja Radgona, the fair 'Dom' (a fair for building construction finishing work) in Ljubljana, the Ljubljana Furniture Fair, the 'Sodobna Elektronika' (contemporary electronics) fair in Ljubljana, the 'Energetika' fair (energy supply and conservation) in Celje, the 'Forma Tool', 'Plag-kem' and 'Grafika' fairs (toolmaking, plastics and graphics) in Celje, as well as the 'Car and Maintenance' and 'Logotrans' fairs (automobile service and repair industry, logistics and transportation) also in Celje.

Opportunities for foreign and domestic exhibitors in future years

Although Slovenia is relatively small, it is the most developed of all 10 countries that will become full members of the European Union in 2004. With its entry into the EU, Slovenia will become even more attractive to many foreign companies for which the quickest and cheapest entry to the Slovenian market will be made possible particularly through fairs. In spite of the fact that from 1 May 2004 Slovenia will be a full EU member, it will still remain a foreign market for all other member countries in certain respects. The free flow of capital, goods and services within the EU will certainly facilitate greatly entry into the Slovenian market, but it will still be necessary to know the cultural peculiarities, economic and political characteristics, language, labour-market situation, sales potential, transportation costs, etc.

When a company makes the decision to enter a foreign market, it can try to manage its business in that market from its headquarters, open an agency abroad, find a sales representative, or participate at international fairs in a foreign country. While the first three methods require a lot of time and financial investment, fairs are the cheapest and the quickest way to research a foreign market and to establish direct contact with customers abroad.

For large companies, too, international trade fairs present a good opportunity for making a first step into the outside world, while for many small and medium-sized companies they are one of the best channels. Trade fairs abroad are the cheapest means of 'testing' foreign markets. It is only at a fair that a company can ascertain at one single location the attitudes of foreign customers, brokers, importers, etc towards their products and services, what the competition has to offer, what the market prices and the channels of distribution are and whether or not it will be necessary to adapt the product or service to the characteristics of the local market. At the fair, a company can quickly and quite cheaply (as compared to other research methods) find out if it is capable of penetrating the market of the country in which the particular fair is held. Of course, it is not easy to develop such information at fairs. Therefore, companies must be sure to send to foreign trade fairs people who will be able to read such information, which means that they must have the necessary product and industry knowledge and a great deal of experience.

Another very great advantage of Slovenian fairs, which will become even more significant after the entry of Slovenia into the EU, is that they not only facilitate entry to the Slovenian market but also to the 20 million people of the countries in the territory of the former Yugoslavia. Slovenian business still has very good economic relations with all these countries. Slovenian people know their language, their culture and their habits. Owing to their economic and political instability, business operations in these countries are still rather risky. However, Slovenian companies, thanks to their good knowledge of the circumstances, are in a better position to deal with the risks. It is exactly for this reason that many companies from Western Europe and the USA decided to grant the agency for all the other countries in the territory of the former Yugoslavia, as well as the agency for Slovenia, to Slovenian companies.

From year to year, more and more visitors come to fairs in Slovenia from Croatia, Bosnia and Herzegovina, Serbia and Montenegro, as well as Macedonia, looking for business contacts and opportunities with Slovenian companies and the companies from the EU that exhibit at Slovenian fairs, either directly or through their agents. Moreover, the number of exhibitors from these countries is increasing as well, since they are aware that, upon Slovenia's entry into the EU, Slovenia will provide them with an excellent bridgehead from which to enter the entire EU market.

Part Five

Appendices

Government Bodies and Other Organizations

Government

British Embassy
Commercial Section
4th Floor
Trg Republike 3
1000 Ljubljana
Tel: + 386 1 200 39 40
Fax: + 386 1 425 90 80
E-mail: info@british-embassy.si

Embassy of the Republic of Slovenia
Economic Section
10 Little College Street
London SW1P 3SH
Tel: + 44 20 7222 5400
Fax: + 44 20 7222 5277
E-mail: metka.urbas@mzz-dkp.gov.si

Institute of Macroeconomic Analysis and Development
Gregorčičeva 27
1000 Ljubljana
Tel: +386 1 478 10 12
Fax: +386 1 478 10 70
E-mail: gp.umar@gov.si
Web site: www.gov.si/zmar

Office of the President of the Republic
Erjavceva 17
SI-1000 Ljubljana
Tel: +386 1 478 12 05
Fax: +386 1 478 13 57

Office of the Prime Minister
Gregorčičeva 20
1000 Ljubljana
Tel: +386 1 478 10 00
Fax: +386 1 478 16 07

Ministry of Economy
Kotnikova 5
1000 Ljubljana
Tel: +386 1 478 36 00
Web site: www.mg-rs.si

Ministry of Finance
Župančičeva 3
1502 Ljubljana
Tel: +386 1 478 52 11
Fax: +386 1 478 56 55
Web site: www.gov.si/mf/

Ministry of Foreign Affairs
Prešernova 25
1000 Ljubljana
Tel: +386 1 478 20 00
Fax: +386 1 478 23 47
Web site: www.gov.si/mzz

Ministry of the Interior
Štefanova 2
1000 Ljubljana
Tel: +386 1 472 51 11
Fax: +386 1 251 43 30
Web site: www.mnz.si

Ministry of Justice
Župančičeva 3
1000 Ljubljana
Tel: +386 1 369 52 00
Fax: +386 1 369 57 83
Web site: www.gov.si/mp

Ministry of Labour, Family and Social Affairs
Kotnikova 5
1000 Ljubljana
Tel: +386 1 478 34 50,
Fax: +386 1 478 34 56
Web site: www.gov.si/mddsz/

Office for European Affairs
Šubičeva 11
1000 Ljubljana
Tel: + 386 1 478 24 25
Fax: + 386 1 478 23 10
Web site: www.gov.si/svez/

Office for Immigration
Riharjeva 38
1000 Ljubljana
Tel: +386 1 283 36 24
Fax: +386 1 283 35 81
E-mail: upb@gov.si

Office for the Prevention of Corruption
Slovenska 54
1000 Ljubljana
Tel: +386 1 434 05 40
Fax: +386 1 434 05 50
E-mail: anti.korupcija@gov.si

Office for Structural Policy and Regional Development
Kotnikova 28
1000 Ljubljana
Tel: +386 1 431 20 50
Fax: +386 1 378 37 60
Web site: www.gov.si/svrp

Public Procurement Office
Slovenska cesta 54
1000 Ljubljana
Tel: +386 1 432 70 46

Statistical Office of the Republic of Slovenia
Vožarski pot 12
1000 Ljubljana
Tel: +386 1 241 51 00
Fax: +386 1 241 53 44
Web site: www.stat.si

TIPO – Slovenian Trade and Investment Promotion Agency
Kotnikova 28
SI-1000 Ljubljana
Tel: + 386 1 478 3557
Fax: + 386 1 478 3599
E-mail: tipo@gov.si
Web site: www.investslovenia.org

Organizations

Bank of Slovenia
Slovenska 35
1505 Ljubljana
Tel: +386 1 471 90 00
Fax: +386 1 251 5516, +386 1 251 55 41
Telex: 31214 BS LJB SI
E-mail: bsl@bsi.si
Web site: www.bsi.si/

Chamber of Commerce and Industry of Slovenia
Dimičeva 13
SI-1504 Ljubljana
Tel: + 386 1 589 80 00
Fax: + 386 1 589 81 00
E-mail: infolink@gzs.si
Web site: www.gzs.si

Employer's Organization of Slovenia
Vita Kraigherja 5
2001 Maribor
Tel: +386 2 231 06 10
Fax: +386 2 250 26 84
E-mail: dos1@siol.net

Ljubljana Stock Exchange, Inc.
Slovenska cesta 56
Ljubljana
Tel: +386 1 471 02 11
Fax: +386 1 471 02 13
E-mail: info@ljse.si
Web site: www.ljse.si

Official Gazette of the Republic of Slovenia
Slovenska cesta 9
SI-1000 Ljubljana
Tel: + 386 1 201 838
Web site: www.uradni-list.si

The Permanent Court of Arbitration
Dimičeva 13
SI-1504 Ljubljana
Tel: + 386 1 598 180/2
Fax: + 386 1 5898 100

Port of Koper
Volkovo Nabrezje 38
SI-6501 Koper
Tel: + 386 5 6656 901
Web site: www.luka-kp.si

Slovenian Insurance Association
Zelezna cesta 14
SI-1000 Ljubljana
Tel: + 386 1 4735 699
Web site: www.zav-zruzenje.si

Slovenia Weekly
Vitrum, Hradeckega 38
SI-1000 Ljubljana
Tel: + 386 1 4261 412
Web site: www.vitrm.si/sw

World Trade Center Ljubljana
Dnajska 156
Sl-1113 Ljubljana
Tel: + 386 1 534 46 66
Web site: www.wtc-lj.si

Appendix 2

Contributor Contact Details

Association of Management Consulting of Slovenia (AMCOS)
Dimiceva 13
Ljubljana S-15045
Slovenia
Tel: +386 1 589 82 54
Fax: +386 1 589 82 00
Email: majda.dobravc@gzs.si
Contact: Majda Dobravc

Bank Austria Creditanstalt
Dr Karl Lueger-Ring 10
1010 Wien
Austria
Tel: + 43 1 53131 41964
Fax: +43 1 53131 41050
E-mail: bernhard.sinhuber@ba-ca.com
Contact: Bernhard Sinhuber

Celjski Sjem d.d. (Celje Fair Plc)
Dečkova 1
3102 Celje
Slovenia
E-mail: robert.otorepec@ce-sejem.si
Contact: Robert Otorepec

Civilitas Research
13 Queen Olga Street
PO Box 16183
2086 Nicosia
Cyprus
Tel: + 357 22 492 555
Fax: + 357 22 496 040
E-mail: james.lindsay@civilitasresearch.com
Contact: Dr James Ker-Lindsay

Coface
12, Cours Michelet
92065 Paris La Défense
Cedex
France
Tel: + 33 149 02 2000
Fax: + 33 149 02 2713

Deloitte & Touche Central Europe
Prievoska 12
821 09 Bratislava
Slovakia
Tel: + 421 258 249 111
Fax + 421 258 249 222
E-mail: rtroch@deloitteCE.com
Contact: Remi Troch

Jadek & Pensa
Tavcarjeva 6
1000 Ljubljana
Slovenia
Tel: + 386 1 234 25 20
Fax: + 386 1 234 25 32
E-mail: pavle.pensa@jadek-pensa-op.si
Contact: Pavle Pensa

The Merchant International Group Limited (MIG)
75–79 Knightsbridge
London SW1X 7RB
Tel: + 44 20 7259 5060
Fax: + 44 20 7254 5090
E-mail: merchantinternational@hotmail.com
Contact: Dr Rashna Writer

Mlinotest
Tovarniska cesta 14, 5270
Ajdovscina
Slovenia
E-mail: jani.toros@mlinotest.si
Contact: Jani Toros

Postna Banka Slovenia d.d.
Vita Krajghrja No 5
2000 Maribor
Slovenia
Tel: + 386 222 88202
Fax: + 386 222 88203
E-mail: gordana.dragic@pbs.si
Contact: Gordana Dragic

Jonathan Reuvid
Little Manor, Wroxton
Banbury, Oxfordshire OX15 6QE
United Kingdom
Tel: + 44 1295 738 070
Fax: + 44 1295 73 090
E-mail: jrwroxton@aol.com

TIPO – Slovenian Trade & Investment Promotion Agency
Kotnikova 28
SI-1000 Ljubljana
Slovenia
Tel: + 386 1 478 35 57
Fax: + 386 1 478 35 99
E-mail: Mateja.Gnidovec@gv.si
Contact: Mateja Gnidovec

Varstroj d.d.
Industrjska Ulica 4
9220 Lendava
Slovenia
Tel: +386 2 578 88 21
Fax: +386 2 575 12 77
Email: janos.orban@varstroj.si
Contact: Janos Orban

Index

Index of Advertisers

Other titles in this series from Kogan Page